The Early Detection of Reading Difficulties:
A Diagnostic Survey with Recovery Procedures

Other books by Marie Clay

Reading: The Patterning of Complex Behaviour
Sand (Concepts About Print Test)
Stones (Concepts About Print Test)
What Did I Write?
Reading Begins at Home (Co-author)

The Early Detection of Reading Difficulties:
A Diagnostic Survey with Recovery Procedures

Marie M. Clay

Professor of Education, University of Auckland

Heinemann Educational Books

Heinemann Educational Books

26 Kilham Avenue, Auckland 9, New Zealand
22 Bedford Square, London WC 1B 3HH, England
4 Front Street, Exeter, New Hampshire 03833, U.S.A.

Also at Edinburgh, Melbourne, Johannesburgh, Ibadan, Nairobi,
Lusaka, New Delhi, Hong Kong, Singapore, Kuala Lumpur,
Kingston, Port of Spain.

ISBN 0 86863 253 8
 SBN 435 80239 9
© 1979 Marie M. Clay
First published 1972
Reprinted 1975, 1976, 1977, 1979
Second edition 1979

Type set by Rennies Illustrations, Auckland
Artwork by Helen Cross Enterprises

The pronouns she and he have often been used in this
text to refer to the teacher and the child respectively.
Despite a possible charge of sexist bias it makes for
clearer, easier reading if such references are
consistent.

Contents

Introduction

My research question in 1962 was 'Can we see the process of learning to read going wrong, close to the onset of reading instruction?' The answer was 'Yes' and by 1972 it was possible to describe for the use of teachers, some of the techniques which were developed for that research programme. The first edition of this book covered only that. Those techniques have been revised and expanded in this new edition and a second test booklet for the Concepts About Print Test has been written. When children are too familiar with *Sand*, teachers can now try them on *Stones*.

Teachers who found the procedures useful in detecting children who were in need of help beyond the classroom programme asked for further guidance. Could we suggest how they should teach these failing children? They were asking for specific procedures which they were not able to invent from the general description in *'Reading: The Patterning of Complex Behaviour'*.

In 1976 the research questions became 'Can we use the collective experience of good teachers to develop and describe some teaching procedures that can be used with failing children in schools?' With the full support of the Department of Education in Auckland, a three year project was undertaken covering both the development and field trials of teaching procedures. These are described in this second edition.

A critical question would relate to the progress of the children. It would not be inconsistent with the theoretical position I had described (Clay, 1979) to find that failing children could be accelerated markedly, providing they were given help early after one year of instruction. But to suggest that many could be returned to average levels of performance was a prediction counter to a wealth of earlier reports and knowledge. A careful research control was kept over the field trials in 1978 and the results are reported in the final part of this book. The results were encouraging. Children made exceptional progress, which reflects favourably on the theory, the reading recovery procedures, and the teachers who helped them.

A note of caution must be sounded. Most (80 to 90 percent) children do *NOT* require these detailed, meticulous, and special reading recovery procedures *or any modification of them*. They will learn to read more pleasurably without them. For a few children individual and consistent tutoring with these special procedures introduced after one year of instruction may well prevent the development of a pattern of reading failure.

The Reading Process

Reading, like thinking, is a very complex process. When you think, all you have to do is produce the responses from within you. When you read you have to produce responses which are precisely the ones the author wrote; you have to match your thinking to his.

You will be familiar with the old game 'Twenty Questions'. Reading is very much like that. The smartest readers ask of themselves the most effective questions for reducing the uncertainty; the poorer readers bumble around with the trivial questions and waste their opportunities to reduce uncertainty. They do not put the information-seeking process into effective sequences.

And many remedial programmes direct their students to the trivial questions. All readers, from the 5-year-old on his first book, to the efficient adult use

- the sense
- the sentence structure
- order
- size
- special features
- special knowledge
- the first and last letter cues

before they resort to left to right sounding out of letters. This is what makes the terms 'look and say', 'sight words' and 'phonics' nonsense as explanations of what we do when we read, and what we need to do in order to be able to read.

By far the most important challenge, for the teacher in reading, is to change the way in which the child *operates* on print to get the message. And because this is basic to the research I want to report, we must look briefly at the model of the reading process that was used.

Reading, naturally involves messages expressed in *language*. Usually it is a special kind of language which is found in books. English-speaking children bring to the reading situation, fluent oral language. This consists of an unconscious control of most of the sounds of the language, a large vocabulary of word labels for meanings that are understood, and strategies for constructing sentences.

Reading also involves direction, space formats, punctuation cues and so on — things which the skilled reader is not even aware of because he responds automatically to such *conventions about print*.

Reading involves *visual patterns* — clusters of words/syllables/blends/letters — however one wants to break the patterns up. The reading process is so automatic in skilled readers that it is only by drastically altering the reading situation that we can show how adults scan text to pick up cues from patterns and clusters of these components. Children tend to operate on visual patterns in very personal ways.

The flow of oral language does not always make the breaks between words clear and children have some difficulty breaking messages into words. They have even greater difficulty in breaking up a word into its sequence of sounds and *hearing* the *sounds in sequence*. This is not strange. Some of us have the same problem with the note sequences in a new melody.

These are four different areas of reading skills, each of which the child can use when reading text. *Language* was put first because the message embodied in print is of high priority. Language has two powerful bases for prediction, its structure and meaning. A useful but sometimes confusing and distorting language base exists in letter-sound relationships.

The *Concepts About Print* was mentioned because although this learning becomes subconscious or automatic it cannot be taken for granted in the early stages. It is sometimes the source of some fundamental confusions.

The *Visual Analysis Skills* were mentioned because visual cues are basic for correct fluent functioning, but skilled readers tend to use visual knowledge in a purely incidental way, just scanning sufficiently to check on the meaning. The beginner reader must discover for himself how to operate in this way.

The *Sound Sequences in Words* are also used in rapid reading to anticipate a word from a few cues or to check a word one is uncertain about. This requires two kinds of detailed analysis in strict coordination: the analysis of the sound sequence and the directional analysis of the visual sequence.

Reading involves the integration of all four sources of cues. The High Progress Reader *even at 6 years*, operates on print in an integrated way with high accuracy and high self-correction rates. He uses a central method of word attack; that is, he reads with attention focussed on meaning. What he thinks the text will say is checked by looking for sound-to-letter associations. He also has several ways of functioning according to the difficulty level of the material. Where he cannot grasp the meaning with higher-level strategies he can engage a low gear and use another strategy such as letter-to-sound knowledge.

On the other hand, the Low Progress Reader or reader 'at risk' has no resource to fall back on. He tends to operate on a narrow range of strategies all the time. He may rely on what he can invent from his memory for the text but pay no attention at all to visual details. He may disregard obvious discrepancies between his response and the words on the page. He may be looking so hard for words he knows and guessing words from first letters that he forgets what the message is about. These unbalanced ways of operating on print can become habituated and automatic when they are practised day after day. They are very resistant to change and this can happen as early as the first 12 to 18 months of instruction.

That is why a Diagnostic Survey after one year of instruction is so important. Intervention at this stage can help the children who are stumbling to operate on print more appropriately so they can continue to progress spontaneously in the classroom. Because each child having difficulty will have different things he can or cannot do, different confusions, different gaps in his item knowledge and different ways of operating on print, each failing child needs an intervention programme especially tailored to his needs in a one-pupil-one-teacher situation.

Reading Recovery Programmes

Since I first began to work with children with learning difficulties more than 30 years ago the teaching problems have remained much the same, although the services have increased and improved and the percentage of children needing help may have been reduced. What we do have today is an awareness of reading difficulties among teachers, parents and the community that did not exist in the 1940s when we were trying to create that awareness.

But with community interest there has been a proliferation of naive ideas about what reading is, and what reading difficulty is. Incorrect and misleading statements are made almost daily — the following are two common examples.

• Critics of the schools often assume that people differ in intelligence but they expect all people to reach a *similar* level in reading. These two expectations are contradictory.
• Completely erroneous statements are made about *words seen in reverse* or *the brain scrambling the signals for the eyes* or *squares looking like triangles*. There is no evidence to support such nonsensical descriptions of how our brains work as we read.

These errors of understanding arise from adults who make superficial or poor observations of their own skills or who disseminate misguided interpretations of new concepts, half-understood.

By the fourth year at school a teacher will have a range of reading ability in her classroom that spreads over about five years. The less able children will read at a Standard One level and the more able children will read above a Form Two level. This describes the expectable *normal range of ability* which the class teacher must provide for. It is the result of differences in intellectual ability, differences in response to schools and to instruction, and differences in life experiences. It is also a product of the amount of successful reading that the child has been able to accumulate.

Teachers and the educational system should make every effort to reduce the number of children falling below their class level in reading, but public opinion must learn to ask different evaluative questions. If all children at every point in the range of normal variation are increasing their skill then the school is doing its job well. All children will not be able to read in the same way any more than they can all think alike.

Let me give an example. Livia had many differences in his preschool experiences compared with the average school entrant. He was over 7 years before he was able to start reading books. In his fourth year at school he was reading well at a lower Standard One or third year level. In one sense he was not a reading problem. His rate of progress *once he had begun to read* was about average. Livia needed reading material and instruction *at his level* so that he could continue to learn to read and only in that sense had he a reading problem. If put on to fifth year materials he would work at frustration level and could even 'go backwards' because he would no longer be practising, in smooth combination, the skills he had developed so far. In this way he could become illiterate for want of appropriate pacing of his reading material. There is a reading level, about an average 10 to 11 year level, below which the child may lose, rather than maintain, his skill when he moves out into the community. If our reading skill is not sufficient for us to practise it every day by reading the paper or notices, or instructions, then we seem to lose some of the skill in much the same way as we lose a foreign language we no longer speak.

A first requirement for a reading recovery programme is that all teachers check the provisions they make for the lowest reading group in their class. Is the programme really catering for the range of reading achievement that was recorded on the survey tests of reading such as the Progressive Achievement Tests of Reading Comprehension and Vocabulary? It is *very* important to ensure that the difficulty level of the reading material is appropriate. If children in a low reading group are not reading for meaning, if what they read does not sound like meaningful language, if they are stuttering over sounds or words with no basis for prediction, they should be taken back to a level of reading material that they can read accurately, with only 1 error in 5 to 10 words. Each classroom needs a wide range of reading books to cater for the expected range of reading skills. Just as you might find it relaxing on holiday to pick up a light novel, an Agatha Christie or a science fiction book, children enjoy easy reading too. *On easy material they practise the skills they have and build up fluency.*

Perhaps one or two children in the lowest group do not seem to be able to read anything. It may be that they have been forced to read at frustration level for as long as a year or two, and that they *have lost their initial reading skills.* Children can go backwards later in their schooling, reading worse than they did at 7 years. Such children may need individual teaching in order to re-develop an independent attack on books.

In the lowest reading group of many classes there could

be a child who has never started to learn to read. Such children need a remedial specialist's attention three or four times a week for two to three years at least and if they are older pupils even this will not make up for those years of lost learning and their associated sense of failure.

What are the ingredients of a good reading recovery programme? For a good recovery programme you need a very experienced teacher who has been trained to think incisively about the reading process and who is sensitive to individual differences.

You need an organization of time and place that permits such teachers to work individually with the children who have the least skills. The teacher helps and supports the pupil in reading meaningful messages in texts which are expertly sequenced to the individual's needs.

The teacher aims to produce in the pupil a set of behaviours which will ensure a self-improving system. With a self-improving set of behaviours the more the reader reads the better he gets, and the more unnecessary the teacher becomes.

The teacher expects to end up with pupils who are as widely distributed in reading as they are in the population in intelligence, mathematical ability, rugby sense, or in cooking prowess. But each pupil should be making progress, from where he is to somewhere else.

Frequently someone approaches me with this kind of statement — 'I am not a teacher, but I would like to help children with reading difficulties. Do you think I could?' My answer is that the best person to help a child with reading difficulties is a trained teacher, who has become a master teacher of reading, and who has been trained as a specialist in reading problems. There is no room for an amateur approach to children with reading difficulties.

And unlike many human conditions failure to read does not end in spontaneous recovery.

Early Intervention

All understandings of how we read, and of what the reading process is, have changed in the last fifteen years under the impact of reports from intensive research efforts. What the older scholars recommend as techniques still have validity; the ways in which they understood the reading process do not. Theorists now look upon the reading process in a different way and that makes many of the older books on reading out of date. It is not enough today to recommend old concepts and cures to solve reading difficulties. We now have very good reasons for discarding old concepts that led to ineffective teaching.

If I believed for example that visual images of words had to be implanted by repetition in children's minds, and that a child had to know every set of letter-sound relationships that occur in English words then I could not explain my successes. I could not explain how an 11-year-old with a reading age of 8 years could make three years progress in reading in six months, having two short lessons each week. It just would not be possible. A good theory ought at least to be able to explain its successes.

When I surveyed the many studies which measured children before remedial work, after the programmes, and then after a follow-up period, the results were almost always the same. Progress was made while the teacher taught, but little progress occurred once the clinical programme finished. There was little progress back in the classroom. One study like this carried out in New Zealand recently had the same result. The children could not continue to progress without the remedial teacher. They were not learning reading in the way that successful readers learn. Successful readers learn a system of behaviours which continues to accumulate skills merely because it operates. (Exceptional reading clinicians do help children to build self-improving strategies but they do not seem to do this frequently enough to influence the research findings.)

We have operated in the past on a concept of remedial tuition that worked but did not work well enough. There have been clinicians, principals, teachers, and willing folk in the community working earnestly and with commitment. Individual children have received help but the size of the problem has not been reduced. Some children were recovered, others were maintained with some improvement and some continued to fail. Why? Lack of early identification has been one reason. In other areas of special education we identify our deaf babies, our blind and cerebral-palsied preschoolers get special help to minimize the consequential aspects of their handicap, but in reading teachers have often waited until the child's third or fourth year at school before selecting children for remedial instruction. By then the child's reading level is two years behind that of his peers. The difficulties of the young child might be more easily overcome if he had practised error behaviour less often, had less to unlearn and relearn, and still had reasonable confidence in his own ability. At the risk of paying too much attention to a few children who would have recovered without special attention, schools must change their organization to solving these problems early. It only takes a child with the most supportive teacher three to four months at school to define himself as 'no good at that' when the timetable comes around to reading activities.

Teachers and parents of 11-to 16-year-olds often believe that schools have done nothing for the reading difficulties of the young people they are concerned about. Yet the older child has probably been the focus of a whole sequence of well-intentioned efforts to help, each of which has done little for the child. This does not mean that we do not sometimes succeed with a brilliant teacher, a fantastic teacher-child relationship, a hard-working parent-child team. What it does mean is that the efforts often fail *for want of experienced teaching, and for want of persistence and continuity of efforts.* They often fail because they are begun too late.

It seemed to me that the longer we left the child failing the harder the problem became and three years was too long. The results of waiting are these.

• There is a great gap or deficit to be made up.
• There are consequential deficits in other aspects of education.
• There are consequences for the child's personality and confidence.
• An even greater problem is that the child has not failed to learn in his three years at school, he has tried to do his work, he has practised his primitive skills and he has habituated, daily, the wrong responses. He has learned; and all that learning stands like a block wall between the remedial teacher and the responses that she is trying to get established. A remedial programme must take what has to be unlearned into account.

Why have we tended to wait until the child was eight or more years old?

• We believed, erroneously, that children mature into reading.
• We do not like to pressure children, and we gave them time to settle.
• We knew children who were 'late bloomers', (or we thought we did).
• Our tests were not reliable until 7:6 years and we were loathe to label children wrongly or to use scarce remedial resources on children who would recover spontaneously.
• We did not understand the reading process sufficiently well.
• We thought a change of method, a search for the great solution, would one day make the reading problem disappear.
• We believed in simple, single causes such as 'not having learned his phonics.'
• Teachers have real difficulty in observing which children are having difficulty at the end of the first year of instruction often claiming there are no such children in their schools.

In 1962 when I began my research I asked the simple question 'Can we see the reading process going wrong in the first year of instruction?' It was, in terms of our techniques at the time an absurd question. The answer is however, that today this can be done by the well-trained teacher. And it is much simpler than administering batteries of psychological tests or trying to interpret the implications for reading of neurological examinations.

At the end of the first year at school, teachers can locate children who can be seen to need extra resources and extra help to unlearn unwanted behaviours or to put together isolated behaviours into a workable system. Simple tests will predict well which young children who have been in instruction for one year, are readers 'at risk'. The test results give the teacher some idea of what to teach next. The second year at school, (from 6 to 7 years in New Zealand) can then be used as a reading recovery year.

The techniques described later in this book were developed in a recent research programme which focussed on the discovery of what strategies good teachers used with slow readers. We were trying to discover, describe and test what approaches work with failing readers at this level. For two years we worked in a clinical programme. Then we tried out the procedures in five very different schools, and revised our ideas of what will work in the school setting. We made a determined effort to reduce reading failure in 122 6-year-olds.

The Sensitive Observation of Reading Behaviour

First steps in the prevention of reading difficulties can be taken in any school system by the sensitive appraisal of the individuality of school entrants, and the careful observation at frequent intervals of children's responsiveness to a good school programme. Whether predictive tests are available or not, the school programme can be organized to provide for the observation and recording of what children are doing. Observation of children's behaviour is a sound basis for the early evaluation of reading progress. Children may stray off into poor procedures at many points during the first year of instruction.

Of 100 children studied in one Auckland-based study there were children making slow progress because of poor language development and whose real problem lay in their inability to form and repeat phrases and sentences. There were many children who wavered for months trying to establish a consistent directional approach to print. There were children who could not hear the separation of words within a spoken sentence, nor the sequence of sounds that occur in words. Some children attended only to the final sounds in words. Two left-handed writers had some persisting problems with direction, but so did several right-handed children. For some children with poor motor coordination the matching of words and spaces with speech was a very difficult task. But other children with fast speech and mature language could not achieve success either, because they could not slow down their speech to their hand speed. They needed help with coordinating their visual perception of print and their fast speech. There were unhappy children who were reticent about speaking or writing, and there were rebellious and baulky children. There were children of low intelligence who made slow progress with enthusiasm, and there were others with high intelligence who worked diligently and yet were seldom accurate. There were those who lost heart when promoted because they felt they were not able to cope, and others who lost heart because they were kept behind in a lower reading group.

A flexible programme which respects individuality at first, gradually brings children to the point where group instruction can be provided for those with common learning needs.

While sensitive observation during the first year of instruction is the responsibility of the class teachers, a survey of reading progress after one year of instruction should be programmed by a person responsible for organization and evaluation within the junior school. Such a survey is held to be desirable and practical, in addition to the activities of class teachers.

A year at school will have given all children a chance to settle, to begin to try their abilities in reading, to be approached by several programmes, to be forming good or bad habits. It is not hurrying children unduly to take stock of their style of progress a year after society introduces them to formal instruction. Indeed, special programmes must then be made available for those children who have been unable to learn from the standard teaching practices. This makes good psychological and administrative sense.

The Early Detection of Reading Difficulties

Traditionally reading difficulties have been assessed with readiness tests, intelligence tests, and tests of related skills such as language abilities or visual discrimination. These have been used to predict areas which might account for a child's reading failure. The problem with the intricate profiles that such tests produce is that while they may sketch some strengths and weaknesses in the child's behaviour repertoire, they do not provide much guide as to what the teacher should try to teach the child *about reading*. The child with limited language skills must still be taught to read, although some authorities advise teachers to wait until the child can speak well. The child with visual perception difficulties can be put on a programme of drawing shapes and finding paths through mazes and puzzles, but he must still be taught to read.

Many research studies have found no benefit resulting from training programmes derived directly from such test results. The pictorial and geometric stimuli used with young retarded readers did not produce gains in reading skill. And oral language training was no more useful. This may well be because the children were learning to analyse data which they did not require in the reading task and they were not learning anything that was directly applicable in the reading activity. Again and again research points to the egocentric, rigid and inflexible viewpoint of the younger, slower or retarded reader. And yet statements on remediation just as often recommend training the child on 'simpler' material — pictures, shapes, letters, sounds — all of which require a large amount of skill to transfer them to the total situation of reading a message which is expressed in sentence form! To try to train children to read on pictures and shapes or even on puzzles, seems a devious route to reading. One would not deny that many children need a wide range of supplementary activities to compensate for barren preschool lives; but it is foolish to prepare for reading by painting with large brushes, doing jig-saw puzzles, arranging large building blocks, or writing numbers. Preparation for reading can be done more directly with written language.

Having established that printed forms are the remedial media, one can then allow that simplification, right down to the parts of the letters, may at times be required for some children (Hooten, 1976). But the larger the *chunks of printed language the child can work with, the quicker he learns,* and the richer the network of meanings he can use. We should only dwell on detail to discover its existence and then to use it when it is absolutely necessary.

There have been many attempts to match teaching methods to the strengths of groups of children. The child with good visual perception is said to benefit from sight-word methods; the child with good auditory perception is thought to make better progress on phonic methods. One author writes, 'Children are physiologically oriented to visual or auditory learning.' Another says, 'Teaching phonics as a relatively "pure" form will place a child at a disadvantage if he is delayed in auditory perceptual ability!' Such instruction would place all children at a severe disadvantage; they would have to learn by themselves many skills that their teachers were not teaching, if they were to become successful readers.

Such matching attempts are simplistic, for English is a complex linguistic system full of irregularities. The way to use a child's strengths and improve his weaknesses is not to work on one or the other but to design the tasks so that he practises the weakness with the aid of his strong ability. Rather than take sides on reading methods which deal either with sounds that are synthesized or with sentences which are analysed, it is appropriate to select reading texts which are simple and yet retain the full power of semantic and syntactic richness, helping the child to apply his strong abilities to their analysis on every level of language.

Close observation of a child's weaknesses will be needed because he will depend on the teacher to structure the task in simple steps to avoid the accumulation of confusions. For one child the structuring may be in the visual perception area. For another it may be in sentence patterns. For a third it may be in the discrimination of sound sequences. For a fourth it may be in directional learning.

It therefore seems appropriate to seek diagnosis of those aspects of the reading process which are weak in a particular child soon after he has entered instruction. The Diagnostic Survey has been used to provide such information for children taught in very different programmes for beginning reading (in New Zealand, Scotland, Australia and U.S.A.). Children in different instruction programmes do not score in similar ways but the Diagnostic Survey provides a framework within which early reading behaviour can be explored irrespective of the method of instruction. What will vary from programme to programme will be the typical scores on the tests of the Survey after a fixed time in instruction.

In what follows some procedures are outlined that have been found useful for the early detection of reading difficulties. Behind these recommendations lies the belief that it is desirable

• to observe precisely what children are saying and doing
• to use tasks that are close to the learning tasks of the classroom (rather than standardized tests of reading)
• to observe what children have been able to learn (not what they have been unable to do)
• to discover what reading behaviours they should now be taught from an analysis of performance in reading texts, not from pictorial or puzzle material, or from normative scores
• to shift the child's reading behaviour from less adequate to more adequate responding, by training on reading tasks rather than training visual perception or auditory discrimination as separate activities.

There is only slight emphasis on scores and quantifying progress. The real value of the Diagnostic Survey is to uncover what a particular child controls and what operations and items he could be taught next.

Reading instruction often focusses on items of knowledge, words, letters and sounds. Most children respond to this teaching in active ways. They search for links between the items and they relate new discoveries to old knowledge. They operate on print as Piaget's children operate on problems, searching for relationships which order the complexity of print and therefore simplify it.

The end-point of early instruction is reached when the children have a self-improving system. This consists of a history of successful reading of books, a set of operations just adequate for reading a more difficult text for the precise words and meanings of the author. In Smith's terms (1978) they have a 'theory of the world' which works, and they are testing that theory and changing it successively as they read more books.

In this Diagnostic Survey an emphasis will be placed on the operations or strategies that are used in reading, rather than on test scores or on disabilities.

The terms *operation* or *strategy* are used for an action initiated by the child to get messages from a text.

A child may have the necessary abilities but may not have learned how to use those abilities in reading. Therefore he will not be observed to use helpful strategies. *He must learn how to ...*

Or a child may have made insufficient development in one ability area (say, motor coordination) to acquire the required strategy (say, directional behaviour) without special help. *He must learn how to in spite of ...*

Again a child may have items of knowledge about letters and sounds and words but be unable to relate one to the other, to employ one as a cross-check on the other. *He must learn how to check on his own learning...*

In any of these instances the task for the reading recovery programme is to get the child to learn to use any and all of the strategies or operations that are necessary to read texts of a given level of difficulty.

There is an important assumption in this approach. Given a knowledge of some items, and a *strategy* which can be applied to similar items to extract messages, the child then has a general way of approaching new items. We do not need to teach him the total inventory of items. Using the strategies will lead the reader to the assimilation of new items of knowledge. Strategies for operating on print are an important part of a self-improving system.

An example may help to clarify this important concept. Teachers through the years have taught children the relationship of letters and sounds. They have, traditionally, shown letters and given children opportunities to associate sounds with those letters. There seemed to be an obvious need to help the child to translate the letters in his book into the sounds of spoken words. And, in some vague way, this also helped the child in his spelling and story writing.

In our studies of children after one year of instruction we found children at risk in reading who could give the sounds of letters but who found it impossible to hear the sound sequences in the words they spoke. They could go *from letters to sounds* but they were unable to check whether they were right or not because they could not hear the sound sequence in the words they spoke. They were unable to go *from sounds to letters*. Being able to carry out the first operation, letters to sounds, probably leads easily to its inverse for many children but for some of our children at risk one strategy did not imply the other.

After six months of special tutoring Tony's progress report at the age of 6:3 emphasizes not the item gains (in Letter Identification or Reading Vocabulary) but the actions or operations that he can initiate. He can analyse some initial sounds in words, uses language cues, has a good locating response, checks his predictions and has a high self-correction rate.

Tony

• (aged 5:9) has some early concepts about directionality and one-to-one correspondence but his low letter identification score and nil scores on word tests mean that he has no visual signposts with which to check his fluent book language.

• (aged 6:0) has made only slight progress in the visual area. In reading patterned text, he relies heavily on language prediction from picture clues and good memory for text, with very little use of visual information. His self-correction behaviour is almost nil, the two corrections made were on the basis of known words.

• (aged 6:3) identifies 37/54 letter symbols, has started accumulating a reading and writing vocabulary and can analyse some initial sounds in words. In reading unpatterned text, he uses language cues, a good locating response, known sight words and some initial sounds to check his predictions. He has a high self-correction rate.

A reading recovery approach which emphasizes the acquisition of reading strategies by-passes questions of reading levels and learning disabilities. It demands the recording of what the child does, on texts of specified difficulty, it refers to the strengths and weaknesses of his strategies, and compares these with a model of the strategies used by children who make satisfactory progress in reading and whose strategies make up a self-improving system.

In a sense it is an economical approach to helping children with reading failure, because it is

• based on the work of experienced class teachers
• based on early identification
• carried out by class teachers of experience
• directed to strategies or operations which generate further *appropriate* behaviour
• directed towards independence in reading with a self-improving system of reading behaviours as the end goal of the programme.

The Diagnostic Survey

When observations of the reading process are taken with very young children those records can be unreliable. One way to increase the reliability of the interpretations that we make from those observations is to make certain that a wide range of observation tasks is used. In this Diagnostic Survey several observation techniques are described. *No one technique is satisfactory on its own.* Teachers are advised to apply as many as possible to the children for whom important instructional decisions must be made. Reducing the scope of our observations increases the risk that we will make erroneous interpretations. For example, the Concepts About Print test should not be used in isolation because it assesses only one aspect of early reading behaviours.

Selection of Children

Taking into account the time a child has been at school, select for further study all those who are not obviously making good progress at the end of their first year of instruction. In New Zealand schools this would be on the child's sixth birthday (6:0). This will probably include 30 to 50 percent of the class. The time required for such a survey must be set against the teaching time that is devoted to failing readers further on in the education system. Principals must become convinced of this preventive need.

There are several reasons why the sixth birthday seems a better checkpoint than the end of the school year in New Zealand schools. This would stagger the testing load throughout the year and would therefore ensure more individual consideration for each child. An end of year survey would be time-consuming and the range of tests applied would tend to be reduced. Class surveys at other times for other reasons will have their own value but should be additional to a systematic check at the end of the first year of instruction.

To teach yourself something about these procedures it would be a good idea to make an individual case study. Select a child who has been in instruction for one year and who is making some progress but is clearly having difficulties, and try out the procedures.

Although these techniques can be used productively with older failing readers it is important to first gain skill in administration and interpretation of the Diagnostic Survey on the young children for whom it was designed.

A Record of Reading Behaviour on Books

Text difficulty: a preliminary note

A graded series of reading books which use natural language texts, such as the *Ready to Read* series, provides a practical ladder of difficulty (although usually there are one or two weak rungs).

- Throughout schooling, reading progress is indicated by satisfactory reading of increasingly difficult texts.
- New strategies emerge almost unnoticed to cope with increases in difficulty level such as justified print, multisyllabic words and literary or scientific text.
- Natural language texts use the frequently occurring words of English over and over again. (This is the principle behind vocabulary tests, and spelling lists like the Arvidson List.)
- Such material uses frequently occurring combinations of sounds found in English words over and over again.
- Therefore if a child is moving up a practical ladder of difficulty on natural language texts with a steady rate of over 90 percent accuracy at the end of a normal teaching contact he will be getting appropriate opportunity to practise both the words he needs to learn and the clusters of sounds that will help him analyse new words.

If we can get reliable measures of how well he reads his reading books this will be important information for planning his day-to-day instruction. Running records, described below, have proved useful in this respect.

The pivotal observation should be a running record of text reading (similar to Goodman and Burke's miscue analysis, 1976). Teachers use running records for instructional purposes, such as

- the evaluation of text difficulty
- the grouping of children
- the acceleration of a child or moving him back to easier material
- the class placement of a new child transferring school.

For a Diagnostic Survey it is wise to obtain a running record on materials at three levels of difficulty;

- the current book (or selection from that book) just completed with 90 to 100 percent accuracy
- a harder text
- an easier text.

These three samples provide valuable insights into *strengths* (on the easier materials) and *weaknesses* (on the more difficult materials).

For the classroom teacher it is preferable to use text materials that are part of her everyday programme, and a visitor to the school (such as a reading adviser, a speech therapist or a school psychologist) should ask the class teacher for the book the child is working on at present, and for her suggestions about texts that are *just a little* harder or easier in her programme.

However, if there are reasons why such judgements are not easily made, for example because the class does not use any recognizably graded sets of materials, the teacher or observer may wish to have a standard set of graded paragraphs. From these the observer can select paragraphs which provide evidence of reading skills on three levels which reveal strengths, and weaknesses.

Taking a running record

Make a record of each child reading his three books or book selections. Use ticks for each correct response and record every error in full. A sample reading of 100 to 200 words from each text is required. This should take about 10 minutes. At the early reading level when the child is reading caption books or first books the sample of words will fall below 100, but if three books are attempted this will be satisfactory.

A suggested format for a Running Record Summary Sheet can be found on page 93 and procedures for calculating accuracy and self-correction rates on page 99 of this book.

Some conventions used for recording

1 Mark every word read correctly with a tick. A record of the first five pages of the *Ready to Read* book *Early in the Morning,* that was 100 percent correct would look like this.

Bill is asleep.	√	√	√
'Wake up, Bill,'	√	√	√
said Peter.	√	√	
Sally is asleep.	√	√	√
'Wake up, Sally,'	√	√	√
said Mother.	√	√	
Father is shaving.	√	√	√

2 Record a wrong response with the text under it.

Child: | home
Text: | house

3 If a child tries several times to read a word, record all his trials.

Child: | here | h— | home
Text: | house | |

4 If a child succeeds in correcting a previous error this is recorded as 'self-correction' (written SC).

Child: | where | we | when | where | SC
Text: | were | | | |
Example 3 is not a self-correction.

5 If no response is given to a word it is recorded with a dash.
Insertion of a word is recorded over a dash.

No response   Insertion
Child: |—   Child: | here
Text: | house   Text: | —

6 An appeal for help from the child is turned back to the child for further effort — 'Try that again' (TTA).

Child: | — | APPEAL | here
Text: | house | TTA |

7 Sometimes the child gets into a state of confusion and it is necessary to extricate him. The most detached method of doing this is to say '*Try that again*', marking TTA on the record. This usually applies to a line, sometimes to a page.

8 If the child baulks, unable to proceed because he is aware he had made an error and cannot correct it, or because he cannot attempt the next word, he is told the word.

Child: | home |
Text: | house | told

9 Repetition is not counted as error behaviour, if it is correct. Often it results in self-correction, and sometimes it is used to confirm a previous attempt. Even so it is useful to record it as it often indicates how much sorting out the child is doing. 'R' standing for repetition, is used to indicate repetition of a word, with R_2 or R_3 indicating the number of repetitions. If the child goes back over a group of words, or returns to the beginning of the line or

sentence in his repetition, the point to which he returns is shown by an arrow.

Child: | Here is the home | R | SC
Text: | Here is the house | |

10   Directional attack on the printed text is recorded by telling the child to 'Read it with your finger'.

Left to right | L → R
Right to left | R → L or ←
Snaking | $\gtrless$
Bottom to top | B → T

Teachers can develop their own conventions for scoring other behaviour which they notice.

A running record from a child who is making many errors is harder to take and score but the rule is to record all behaviour, and analyse objectively what is recorded.

Reliability

Taped recordings of such reading observations taken from four children over the period of one year were available and were used to check on the reliability of such records (0.98 for error scoring and 0.68 for self-correction scoring, Clay 1966).

A number of trends became obvious during these reliability tests.

- For beginning readers, observers can take running records which give reliable accuracy scores with a small amount of training.
- The effect of poor observation is to reduce the number of errors recorded and increase the accuracy rate. As the observer's skill in recording at speed increases, so the error scores tend to rise.
- To record all error behaviour in full, as against only tallying its occurrence, takes much more practice (but provides more evidence of the child's strategies).
- Observations for poor readers require longer training to reach agreement on scoring standards because of the complex error behaviour.
- Information is lost in the taped observation, especially motor behaviour and visual survey, but observation of vocal behaviour tends to be improved.
- Reliability probably drops as reading-accuracy level falls because there is more error behaviour to be recorded in the same time span.

For research work the most reliable records would be obtained by scoring an observation immediately following its manual recording, and re-checking immediately with a taped observation.

Analysing the reading record

From the running record of reading behaviour containing all the child's behaviour on his current book, consider what is happening as the child reads.

Some conventions for scoring the records

In counting the number of errors, some arbitrary decisions must be made but the following have been found workable.

1   Credit the child with any correct or corrected words.
Child: | to the shops | Errors: 2
Text: | for the bread |
Score: ×   √   ×

2   There is no penalty for trials which are eventually correct.
Child: | Want | won't | went | (SC) Errors: 0
Text: | Went | | | Self-correction: 1
Score: —   —   √

Child: | Where | we | when | were | (SC) Errors: 0
Text: | were | | | | Self-correction: 1
Score: —   —   —   √

3   Insertions add errors so that a child can have more errors than there are words in a line.
Child: | The engine went toot, toot, toot | Errors: 5
Text: | The little engine sighed |
Score: √   ×   ×   ×   ×   ×

4   But a child cannot receive a minus score for a page. The lowest page score is 0.

5   Omissions. If a line or sentence is omitted each word is counted as an error. If a page is omitted (perhaps because two pages were turned together) they are not counted as errors. Note that, in this case, the number of words on that page must be deducted from the Running Words Total before calculation.

6   Repeated errors. If the child makes an error (e.g. 'run' for 'ran') and then substitutes this word repeatedly, it counts as an error every time; but substitution of a proper name (e.g. 'Mary' for 'Molly') is counted only the first time.

7   Multiple errors and self-corrections. If a child makes two or more errors (e.g. reads a phrase wrongly) each word is an error. If he then corrects all these errors each corrected word is a self-correction.

8 Broken words. Where a word is pronounced as two words (e.g. a/way) this is regarded as an error of pronunciation not as a reading error unless what is said is matched to a different word. Such things as 'pitcher' for 'picture' and 'gonna' for 'going to' are counted as correct.

9 Inventions defeat the system. When the young child is creatively producing his own version of the story the scoring system finally breaks down and the judgement 'inventing' is recorded for that page, story or book.

10 'Try that again'. When the child is in a tangle this instruction, which does not involve teaching, can be given. It counts as one error and only the second attempt is scored.

11 Fewest errors. If there are alternate ways of scoring responses a general principle is to choose the method that gives the *fewest* possible errors as in B below.

A   *Child:* | *We went for the bread*
    Text: | You went to the shop for the bread
    Score: × √ × √ × × × ×

                                      Errors: 6

B   *Child:* | *We went   for the bread*
    Text: | You went to the shop for the bread
    Score: × √ × × × √ √ √

                                        Errors: 4

Check directional movement

Ask the child to *'Read it with your finger'*. Three groups of children have difficulty as beginning readers in disciplining their behaviour within the directional constraints of written language.

● The first group are children who have poor motor coordination or who are inattentive to where their bodies are and how they are arranging their movements.
● The second group are fast-reacting, impulsive children who act before they think and who have great difficulty in governing their response within any constraints. They can very readily settle into undesirable patterns of responding.
● A third group of beginners at risk are those who do not like to try because they might make a mistake. The development of directional behaviour involves exploring two-dimensional space, being wrong, and discovering

how to behave correctly. Children who are too tense, inhibited or timid, may be reluctant to try out a range of directional behaviour, discarding the poor responses and retaining the good ones.

Children who have poor motor coordination, who are quick and impulsive, and who are timid, require more time and sensitive teaching to establish directional behaviour. Re-teaching the child who has already failed is even more critical and more difficult. These children are very easily confused, so the teacher must give clear demonstrations with few words, and supervised opportunities for practice with positive reinforcement for behaviour which is close to that required. Without supervision the child will revert to his old habits. Yet this must be prevented. At first the teacher should control the directional behaviour by pointing to beginning letters, words and lines for the child. She may use masking sheets exposing only a few cues at a time in the correct sequence. She must spend longer on this learning than is usually necessary in beginning reading because it must be *overlearned* in order to displace the established learning. When she transfers the control of directional behaviour back to the child the teacher must still monitor his response closely.

As a correction procedure for directional errors teachers should not be afraid to encourage hand action to assist reading. Watch the child as his hand guides his reading and his directional behaviour becomes more stable in

● establishing a top-left starting point
● consistent left to right movement across lines
● matching words in speech to words in text, one after the other
● locating the first letter of lines
● locating the first letter of words.

For the most difficult cases, passively move the child's hand and arm through the appropriate directional movements until he can manage without this guidance.

As correct responding becomes more reliable the teacher can begin to require phrasing and fluency. As this is stressed, finger-pointing will be dropped by the child. But he will regress to old habits

● when a text is new and difficult
● when he is tired
● when the layout is unusual
● when he is incorporating some new aspect of behaviour into his established system of reading behaviour.

Record comments on directional movement on the Diagnostic Survey Summary Sheet (page 95).

Calculate the error rate

Compare the number of errors with the number of running words. Does the child read his book with one error in every three running words of text (which is poor) or is it more like one in twenty (which is good)? Record on the Diagnostic Survey Summary Sheet.

Calculate the percentage of errors (see Conversion Table page 99). If there is more than 10 percent of error in the record rate this is a 'hard' text for this child. (For the average child there is movement from 90 percent accuracy when he is first promoted to a book to 95 percent or more as he completes his learning on that book.)

When the child reads a book with less than 90 percent accuracy it is difficult for him to judge for himself whether his attempt at a word is a good one or a poor one. He needs easier material which he can attempt at a rate of not more than one error in ten words at the time he begins the new book. The reading text should use language that comes readily to him. In the very earliest stages it is sometimes necessary to repeat the text until he has almost memorized it, but not quite. Then it will come readily to the tip of his tongue. It is as if the words he needs are stored in the depths of his memory and have to be assisted to float to the surface. The child's own dictated stories provide good reading texts for just this reason — the words and construction of the text should be readily recalled.

If the text is in a different style from that which the child usually reads his error rate will increase because he is predicting from the baseline of old expectations which are inappropriate for the present text.

Error behaviour

To read a continuous text the child must use a variety of skills held in delicate balance. Specific weaknesses or strengths can upset that balance. There are some questions about the errors for a particular child that can guide the teacher's analysis of the behaviour record. (See also Clay, 1979.)

Oral language skills. Are these good enough to make the reading of this text possible? (For instance, could the child repeat the sentences of the text if you asked him to, one by one?) Or, is his language so fluent that the co-ordination of visual perception and motor movement with language is difficult?

Speed of responding. The rate at which a child reads and the time spent on pausing and processing cues are at this level poor indicators of the child's progress. One child may read with the fluency of oral language but may be a poorer reader than another child who pauses and engages in much self-correction behaviour. At this particular stage in reading progress it is good for the child making average progress to be concerned about error and to rectify error if possible. It is poor to maintain fluency and not to notice that one has made an error.

Fast responding can be an indication that language is dominating the process while little visual search is taking place.

What cues does he depend on? Does the child use meaning? If what he reads makes sense, even though it is inaccurate then he is probably applying his oral language knowledge to his reading.

• Is what he says grammatical? If it is, his oral language is influencing his responding. If it is not, there may be two reasons. Perhaps his language skill is limited and his personal 'grammar' does not contain the structures used in his reading book. Or, if he is paying close attention to detail, or to word by word reading, he may not be allowing his control over English syntax to influence his choices.
• Does he use visual cues from the letters and words?
• Does he read word by word as if recalling each word from a memory bank, unrelated to what has gone before? He may not realize that reading is like speaking, and that his language behaviour is a rich source of help in choosing correct reading responses.

Enter comments on the Analysis of Errors. (Diagnostic Survey Summary Sheet.)

Cross-checking strategies

Can the child check one kind of information with another? Can he get movement and language occurring together in a linked or coordinated way? Does he check on language prediction by looking at some letters? Can he hear the sounds in a word and check whether the expected letters are there? A child with outstanding memory for what he hears or with very fast language production often has difficulty in slowing up enough to enable him to learn the visual discriminations. Yet good readers search for cues from different sources which confirm a response. (See pages 57 to 59 and Clay 1979 for further discussion of these reading behaviours.)

Self-correction

Observe and enter in the running record any self-correction behaviour. The child discovers cues that tell him something is wrong. He is aware that a particular message is to be communicated and tries to discover this by using cues. Efficient self-correction behaviour is an important skill in good reading. A self-correction rate of one in three or five errors is good, but one in twenty errors is a very low rate, the prognosis is good.

If self-correction is evident but inefficient it is a good prognosis. Its absence in a record which contains errors is a danger sign. A child who is making errors and is not aware of this, or who makes no attempt to correct himself, is in difficulties. He is not aware of the need to decode a precise message. He is not aware of the existence of cues or does not know how to use them.

If a child engages in a confusion of unsuccessful attempts to solve his errors he needs to learn better bases for making his decisions. His teacher must deliberately teach some priorities like *'Sound the first letter'*, *'Go back to the beginning of the line'*, *'What would make sense?'* — whichever she judges to be the technique with the highest pay-off in terms of progress, for this child at this time.

Response to I like the swing. I shall get on it. The swing went up and down. It went ...	Interpretation of Behaviour		
	Tries	**Decides**	**Reasons**
I like the swing	Correct		
I shall ke — get	Anticipates wrongly	Corrects	Letter cue?
off it — on it	Anticipates wrongly	Corrects	Meaning?
The swing will — No!	First letter cue	Rejects	Word form?
wa — want	Three letters similar	Rejects	Meaning?
won't (up) — No!	Grammar cue 'The swing won't. . .' plus three letters	Rejects	Following grammar 'won't up'?
will take	New idea	Rejects	One pattern for two responses
we — *wa — No*	A more analytic approach	Rejects	Sounds do not aid recall
(I get mixed up)		'I am confused'	There is always some cue that does not fit
(I'll read it again)	A new approach	Return to the line beginning	'A clean slate'
The swing want	It looks like 'want'	Rejects	Meaning?
*won't up and down	It looks like 'won't'	*Accepts	Fits letter and meaning cues and previous grammar
It — (I get mixed up)	Recognizes the same word	I am confused. Start again	
It won't	Tries previous solution	Rejects	
went(?)	Tries correct sound 'e'	I do not recognize this word	There has been too much error
(I don't know that word)	Gives up	Appeals for help	No more ideas

Letter Identification

What letters does the child know? Which letters can he identify? It is not sufficient to say that he knows 'a few letters'. His tuition should take into account exactly what he knows. (This testing should take 5 to 10 minutes.)

• Test all letters, lower case and capital. The large print alphabet that is printed in this book should be used. It could be removed from the book and mounted on a clipboard for this purpose. Ensure that the child reads *across* the lines so that the letters are treated in a random order.
• Use the Letter Identification Score Sheet (see Appendix). Mark A for an alphabetic response, S for sound, or W for word beginning similarly, and record the incorrect responses.
• Score as correct
— an alphabet name
— a sound that is acceptable for that letter
— a response which says '. . . *it begins like* . . .' giving a word for which that letter is the initial letter.

The scores given below apply when any one of these three criteria of a correct response are used.

Obtain sub-totals for each kind of response, alphabetic, sound or word beginning similarly, and note down
• the child's preferred mode of identifying letters
• the letters a child confuses so that they can be kept apart in the teaching programme
• the unknown letters.

Administration
Use only the following questions to get the child to respond to the letters. *Do not ask only for sounds, or names:*

To introduce the task:
• What do you call these?
• Can you find some that you know?

Pointing to each letter:
• What is this one?

If the child does not respond:
• Do you know its name?
• What sound does it make?
• Do you know a word that starts like that?

Then moving to other letters:
• What is this? And this?

If the child hesitates start with the first letter of his name, and then go to the first line. Point to every letter in turn working across the lines. Use a masking card if necessary.

Following such testing, teaching should aim to improve the child's ability to distinguish letters one from another on any basis that works (not necessarily by letter-sound relationships). Expand the child's range of known letters allowing any distinction that works for that child. As more and more letters are controlled he becomes ready for systematic associations like alphabetic names and sound equivalents which can supplement the original association he chose.

The following tables show scores on Letter Identification as Stanine scores for three large samples of

Research Group	Letter Identification (Normalized Scores — Stanine Groups)								
320 urban children aged 5:0 - 7:0 in 1968	**Stanine group** 1	2	3	4	5	6	7	8	9
	Test score —	0	2-7	8-25	26-47	48-52	53	54	—
282 urban children aged 6:0 - 7:3 in 1978	**Stanine group** 1	2	3	4	5	6	7	8	9
	Test score 0-13	14-28	29-43	44-49	50-52	53	—	54	—

Reliability: 100 urban children aged 6:0 in 1966, 0.97, split-half.
Validity: Correlation with Word Reading for 100 children at 6:0 in 1966, 0.85.

A	F	K	P	W	Z
B	H	O	J	U	
C	I	L	Q	M	
D	N	S	X	I	
E	G	R	V	T	
a	f	k	p	w	z
b	h	o	j	u	a
c	y	l	q	m	
d	n	s	x	i	
e	g	r	v	t	g

children aged 5 to 7 years. (Stanines distribute scores according to the normal curve in nine groups from 1 — the lowest — to 9; Lyman, 1963.) As it is possible for young children to completely master this particular set of learning one would expect a child to move through the Stanine score range until he reached perfect scoring for the symbols of the alphabet.

For comparison choose the research group that best represents the group of children you will be testing.

Letter Identification scores are very sensitive to instructional procedures. The teaching of letter-sound relationships will result in most responses being sounds rather than names, and the whole set of letters may be learned earlier than under a different method of instruction. The 1968 sample of New Zealand children of mixed race was slower to learn Letter Identification responses than another sample tested in 1972.

Concepts About Print

A check (5 to 10 minutes) should be made on significant concepts about printed language. Some of these are: the front of the book, that print (not the picture) tells the story, what is a letter? what is a word? what is the first letter in a word? big and little letters, the function of the space, uses of punctuation (fullstop, question mark, talking marks).

Do not assume that verbal explanation has taught the eyes to locate, recognize and use this information.

The 'Concepts About Print' tests are entitled 'Sand' (Clay, 1972), and 'Stones' (Clay, 1979), and can be used with the 'new entrant' or the 'non-reader' because the child is asked to help the examiner by pointing to certain features as the examiner reads the book. 5-year-old children have some fun and little difficulty with the test items. The test reflects changes in reading skill during the first year of instruction but is of less significance in the subsequent years for children who make average progress. For problem readers confusions about these arbitrary conventions of our written language code tend to persist.

Administration
The tasks present a standard situation within which the child can be observed. Try to retain a standard task but be flexible enough to communicate the task to the child.

Administer the items according to the instructions given. If the child fails item 10, items 12 to 14 are likely to be failed and can be given at the discretion of the examiner. However, items 15 to 24 should be administered to all children.

The instructions for the administration and scoring of this test have been printed on pages 19 to 21.

Interpretation of scores
Score items as instructed on the sheet in this book. Use one of the tables below to convert these to a Stanine score.

Choose the first table if you are assessing 5-year-olds, or if the average Stanine score of 5, seems to fit with

Research Group	Concepts About Print (Normalized Scores — Stanine Groups)								
320 urban children aged 5:0-7:0 in 1968	Stanine score	1	2	3	4	5	6	7	8	9
	Test score	0	1-4	5-7	8-11	12-14	15-17	18-20	21-22	23-24
282 urban children aged 6:0-7:3 in 1978	Stanine score	1	2	3	4	5	6	7	8	9
	Test score	0-9	10-11	12-13	14-16	17-18	19	20-21	22	23-24

Reliability: 40 urban children aged 5:0 to 7:0 in 1968, 0.95, KR.
Validity: Correlation with Word Reading for 100 children at 6:0 in 1966, 0.79.

56 kindergarten children in Texas 1978.
Test-retest reliability coefficients 0.73-0.89
Corrected split-half coefficients 0.84-0.88   (Day and Perkins, 1979)

average progress in your school. Choose the second table if you are assessing 6-year-olds or if the children tend to move more quickly than some other schools in this test area.

A Stanine score is a normalized standard score of nine units, with 1 a low score and 9 a high score. An individual child's Stanine score indicates his status relative to all children in the age group 5:0 to 7:0. It is useful to contrast a particular child's scores after an interval to reflect progress.

It is also useful for a school to build up its own table of Stanine scores. (Lyman, 1963.)

As the 'Concepts About Print' are a limited set of information which can be learned in the first two years of school, young children will test low early in their schooling and their Stanine score should increase as their reading improves.

However the test's greatest value is diagnostic. Items should uncover concepts to be learned or confusions to be untangled. For remedial purposes examine the child's performance and teach the unknown concepts. The items are not in a strict difficulty sequence, but some indication of difficulty is given by the 'Age Expectations for Items' table which gives the age at which average children passed each item. (However, such data will be very dependent on the teaching programme and method-emphasis used in any particular school.)

Scoring Standards

Item	Pass	Score
1	Front of book.	
2	Print (not picture).	
3	Points top left at 'I took...'	
4	Moves finger left to right on any line.	
5	Moves finger from the right-hand end of a higher line to the left-hand end of the next lower line, or moves down the page.	
6	Word by word matching.	
7	Both concepts must be correct, but may be demonstrated on the whole text or on a line, word or letter.	
8	Verbal explanation, or pointing to top of page, or turning the book around.	
9	Score for beginning with 'The' and moving right to left across the lower line and then the upper line, OR, turning the book around and moving left to right in the conventional movement pattern.	
10	Any explanation which implies that line order is altered.	
11	Says or shows that a left page precedes a right page.	
12	Notices at least one change of word order.	
13	Notices at least one change in letter order.	
14	Notices at least one change in letter order.	
15	Says 'Question mark', or 'A question', or 'Asks something'.	
16	Says 'Full stop', or 'It tells you when you've said enough' or 'It's the end'.	
17	Says 'A little stop,' or 'A rest', or 'A comma'.	
18	Says 'That's someone talking', 'Talking', 'Speech marks'.	
19	Locates two capital and lower case pairs.	
20	Points correctly to both *was* and *no*.	
21	Locates one letter and two letters on request.	
22	Locates one word and two words on request.	
23	Locates both a first and a last letter.	
24	Locates one capital letter.	

Age Expectations For Items
(Age at which 50 percent of average European children pass an item)

Age / Item	5:0	5:6	6:0	6:6	7:0			5:0	5:6	6:0	6:6	7:0
1		x					13				x	
2	x						14					x
3		x					15				x	
4		x					16					x
5		x					17					x
6		x					18					x
7		x					19			x		
8		x					20			x		
9		x					21		x			
10		x					22			x		
11		x					23				x	
12				x			24				x	

Concepts About Print Test

Administration and scoring

Before starting, thoroughly familiarize yourself with this test. Use the exact wording given below in each demonstration.

Say to the child, *'I'm going to read you this story but I want you to help me.'*

Cover

Item 1 Test: For orientation of book. Pass the booklet to the child holding the book vertically by outside edge, spine towards the child.

 Say: *'Show me the front of this book.'*

 Score: 1 point for each correct response.

Pages 2/3

Item 2 Test: Concept that print, not picture, carries the message.

 Say: *'I'll read this story. You help me. Show me where to start reading. Where do I begin to read?'*

Read the text.

 Score: 1 for print. 0 for picture.

Pages 4/5

Item 3 Test: For directional rules.

 Say: *'Show me where to start.'*

 Score: 1 for top left.

Item 4 Say: *'Which way do I go?'*

 Score: 1 for left to right.

Item 5 Say: *'Where do I go after that?'*

 Score: 1 for return sweep to left.

(Score items 3-5 if all movements are demonstrated in one response.)

Item 6 Test: Word by word pointing.

 Say: *'Point to it while I read it.'* (Read slowly, but fluently.)

 Score: 1 for exact matching.

Page 6

Item 7

Test: Concept of first and last.
Read the text.
Say: *'Show me the first part of the story.'*
'Show me the last part.'
Score: 1 point if BOTH are correct in any sense, i.e. applied to the whole text or a line, a word or a letter.

Page 7

Item 8

Test: Inversion of picture.
Say: *'Show me the bottom of the picture.'*
(Do NOT mention upside-down.)
Score: 1 for verbal explanation, OR, for turning the book around.

Pages 8/9

Item 9

Test: Response to inverted print.
Say: *'Where do I begin?'*
'Which way do I go?'
'Where do I go after that?'
Score: 1 for beginning with 'The' **(Sand)**, or 'I' **(Stones)**, and moving right to left across the lower and then the upper line. OR 1 for turning the book around and moving left to right in the conventional manner.
Read the text now.

Pages 10/11

Item 10

Test: Line sequence.
Say: *'What's wrong with this?'* (Read immediately the bottom line first, then the top line. Do NOT point.)
Score: 1 for comment on line order.

Pages 12/13

Item 11

Test: A left page is read before a right page.
Say: *'Where do I start reading?'*
Score: 1 point for left page indication.

Item 12

Test: Word sequence
Say: *'What's wrong on this page?'*
(Point to the page number 12 — NOT the text.)
Read the text slowly as if it were correct.
Score: 1 point for comment on either error.

Item 13

Test: Letter order.
Say: *'What's wrong on this page?'*
(Point to the page number 13 — NOT the text.)
Read the text slowly as if it were correct.
Score: 1 point for any ONE re-ordering of letters that is noticed and explained.

Pages 14/15

Item 14

Test: Re-ordering letters within a word.
Say: *'What's wrong with the writing on this page?'*
Read the text slowly as if it were correct.
Score: 1 point for ONE error noticed.

Item 15

Test: Meaning of a question mark.
Say: *'What's this for?'* (Point to or trace the question mark with a finger or pencil.)
Score: 1 point for explanation of function or name.

Pages 16/17

Test: Punctuation.
Read the text.
Say: *'What's this for?'*

Item 16

Point   to or trace with a pencil, the full stop.

Item 17

Point   to or trace with a pencil, the comma.

Item 18

Point   to or trace with a pencil, the quotation marks.

Item 19

Test: Capital and lower-case correspondence.

Say: *'Find a little letter like this.'*
Sand: Point to capital T and demonstrate by pointing to Tt if the child does not succeed.
Stones: As above for Ss.

Say: *'Find a little letter like this.'*
Sand: Point to capital M, H in turn.
Stones: Point to capital T, B in turn.

Score: **Sand:** 1 point if BOTH Mm and Hh are located.
Stones: 1 point if BOTH Tt and Bb are located.

Pages 18/19

Item 20   Test: Reversible words.
          Read the text.
          Say: *'Show me* was.'
              'Show me no.'
          Score: 1 point for BOTH correct.

Page 20

Ensure you have two pieces of light card (13 x 5cm) that the child can hold and slide easily over the line of text to block out words and letters. To start, lay the cards on the page but leave all print exposed.

Item 21   Test: Letter concepts.
          Say: *'This story says [1]"The waves splashed in the hole" (or [2]"The stone rolled down the hill"). I want you to push the cards across the story like this until all you can see is just one letter.'* (Demonstrate the movement of the cards but do not do the exercise.)
          Say: *'Now show me two letters.'*
          Score: 1 point if BOTH are correct.

Item 22   Test: Word concept.
          Say: *'Show me just one word.'*
              'Now show me two words.'
          Score: 1 point if BOTH are correct.

Item 23   Test: First and last letter concepts.
          Say: *'Show me the first letter of a word.'*
              'Show me the last letter of a word.'
          Score: 1 point if BOTH are correct.

Item 24   Test: Capital letter concepts.
          Say: *'Show me a capital letter.'*
          Score: 1 point if correct.

Word Tests

Standardized word tests are based on the principle of sampling from the child's reading vocabulary. They cannot be reliable until the child has acquired sufficient vocabulary to make sampling a feasible strategy.

For early identification a different approach is required. Word lists can be compiled from the high frequency words in the reading materials that are adopted. The principle here is a sampling from the high frequency words of that restricted corpus that the child has had the opportunity to learn. The following test works well for children who are using the *Ready to Read* series.

1 **Sand**   2 **Stones**

'Ready to Read' Word Test

It was found for Auckland children that a small list of 15 words compiled from the 45 most frequently occurring words in the 12 little books of the *Ready to Read* series, was a very good instrument for ranking or grouping children during *the first year* of instruction and for retarded readers in the second year (Clay, 1966). This test, which takes about 2 minutes to administer, can be removed and mounted on a clipboard for easy administration. (It should be noted that any test of first year instruction must be closely linked to that instruction. The most frequently occurring words in whatever basic reading texts are being used will probably provide a satisfactory source of test items.)

Administration

Ask a child to read *one* list. Give List A *or* List B *or* List C. Help the child with the practice word if necessary and never score it. Do not help with any other words and do not use the list for teaching. Use alternate lists for retesting.

Use of the Test

The score will indicate the extent to which a child is accumulating a reading vocabulary of the most frequently used words in the *Ready to Read* series during his first year at school.

The scores may be used for ranking or grouping children (together with teachers' observations recorded for book reading). Successive tests will indicate whether a progressive change is occurring in the child's reading skill.

Score

The following table shows scores on the *Ready to Read* Word Test as Stanine scores for a large sample of children aged 5 to 7 years. (Stanines distribute scores according to the normal curve in nine groups from 1, the lowest, to 9.) It is possible for children to completely master this learning. One would therefore expect a child to move through the Stanine score range until he reached perfect scoring.

What the Test does not do:

• It does not give a reading age.
• It does not discriminate between better readers after one year of instruction. On the contrary it groups them together.
• Differences of less than three score points are not sufficiently reliable to support any decisions about the child's progress, without other evidence.
• It does not sample a child's reading skill if he is working beyond the level of the first twelve books of the *Ready to Read* series.

Research Group	'Ready to Read' Word Test (Normalized Scores — Stanine Groups)									
320 urban children aged 5:0-7:0 in 1968	Stanine group	1	2	3	4	5	6	7	8	9
	Test score	0	0	1	2-5	6-12	13-14	—	15	—
282 urban children aged 6:0-7:3 in 1978	Stanine group	1	2	3	4	5	6	7	8	9
	Test score	0-1	2-5	6-9	10-12	13-14	—	15	—	—

Reliability: 100 urban children aged 6:0 in 1966, 0.90, KR.

Validity: Correlation was 0.90 for Word Test at 6:0 with Schonell R1 at 7:0 for 87 children.

Other Reading Tests

Once the child who entered school at 5 years has a reading level of 6:0 to 6:6 several standardized tests can be applied. A word test, like the Schonell R1, the Southgate Group Reading Test or the Burt-Word Reading Test (1974), will not describe the child's integrated system of reading behaviour because this can only be observed on continuous text. It will rank the child in relation to other children on reading vocabulary.

The Schonell test has been used in many New Zealand studies because it was clearly demonstrated that the score for the Word Test of 15 words (just described) can be added to the score for the first 30 words of the Schonell R1 test to give a combined score which is psychometrically a good measure of reading between 5 and 7 years for New Zealand children.

On the other hand, a paragraph reading test, like the Neale Analysis of Reading Ability, will permit observations of the child's ongoing behaviour, in a situation which is standard and which is graded in difficulty. A teacher who has thought about the reading process can extract much more information about the child's system of operating on cues in reading from a running record on a paragraph reading test than is yielded only by the test scores on this test.

For children whose reading level is above the average after two years of instruction, the Gap Reading Comprehension Test can be used as a paragraph reading test with groups. It provides some evidence of the children's use of meaning and grammatical structure cues.

Writing

Examine examples of the child's writing behaviour. Does he have good letter formation? How many letter forms does he use? Does he have a stock of words which he can construct from memory with the letters correctly sequenced? What are they?

A poor writing vocabulary may indicate that, despite all his efforts to read, a child is in fact taking very little notice of visual differences in print. He requires an all-out effort to induce more writing behaviour to correct for his faulty visual perception. In learning, the hand *and* eye support and supplement each other, organizing the first visual discriminations. Only later does the eye become a solo agent and learning become faster than at the hand-eye learning stage.

Writing samples

A rating technique for stories
Use this kind of appraisal for the early reading stage. Take three samples of the child's stories on consecutive days or for three successive weeks and rate them for language level, message quality and directional features. (One sample is not sufficiently reliable for this evaluation technique.)

LIST A	LIST B	LIST C
Practice Word the	Practice Word said	Practice Word is

I	and	Father
Mother	to	come
are	will	for
here	look	a
me	he	you
shouted	up	at
am	like	school
with	in	went
car	where	get
children	Mr.	we
help	going	they
not	big	ready
too	go	this
meet	let	boys
away	on	please

	A Language Level	B Message Quality	C Directional Principles
Not yet satisfactory	1-4	1-4	1-4
Probably satisfactory	5-6	5-6	5-6

Language level
Record the number of the highest level of linguistic organization used by the child.

1 Alphabetic (letters only).
2 Word (any recognizable word).
3 Word group (any two-word phrase).
4 Sentence (any simple sentence).
5 Punctuated story (of two or more sentences).
6 Paragraphed story (two themes).

Message quality
Record the number below for the best description of the child's sample.

1 He has a concept of signs (uses letters, invents letters, uses punctuation).
2 He has a concept that a message is conveyed.
3 A message is copied.
4 Repetitive use of sentence patterns like 'Here is a...'
5 Attempts to record own ideas.
6 Successful composition.

Directional principles
Record the number of the highest rating for which there is no error in the sample of the child's writing.

1 No evidence of directional knowledge.
2 Part of the directional pattern is known:
   Either start top left
   Or move left to right
   Or return down left.
3 Reversal of the directional pattern (right to left and return down right).
4 Correct directional pattern.
5 Correct directional pattern and spaces between words.
6 Extensive text without any difficulties of arrangement and spacing of text.

A test of writing vocabulary

A test of writing vocabulary, constructed by Susan M. Robinson (1973) was included in the test battery of her research on predicting early reading progress. Hildreth (1964) and de Hirsch et al (1966) had suggested that writing behaviour was a good indicator of a child's knowledge of letters, and of left to right sequencing behaviour. In writing words letter by letter the child must recall not only the configuration but also the details. Children's written texts are a good source of information about a child's visual discrimination of print for as the child learns to print words, hand and eye support and supplement each other to organize the first visual discriminations.

A test was constructed where the child was encouraged to write down all the words he knew how to write, starting with his own name and including basic vocabulary and words personal to the child. This simple test was both reliable (i.e. a child tended to score at a similar level when retested two weeks later) and valid in the sense that it had a high relationship with word reading scores.

The distribution of scores changes markedly when a group of 5:6-year-olds is compared with two groups of 6-year-olds in the graph (page 25).

There is probably a high degree of interdependence between reading words and writing words. Writing ability and word reading ability may both be the result of many kinds of experience with letters, numbers, words, stories and drawings which have enabled the child to learn many things about print. It should not be assumed from this that success in the first years of learning to read would be assured by simply teaching children to write words.

Administration and scoring
Give the child a blank piece of paper and a pencil and then say *'I want to see how many words you can write. Can you write your name?'* (Start ten minute timing here.)
If the child says 'No', ask him if he knows any single letter or two letter words.
   'Do you know how to write is? to? I? or a?'
If the child says 'Yes' say
   'Write your name for me.'
When the child finishes say
   'Good. Now think of all the words you know how to write and write them all down for me.'
Give the child up to 10 minutes to write words he knows. When he stops writing, or when he needs prompting,

suggest words that he might know how to write.

'Do you know how to write I or a?'
'Do you know how to write is or to?'

Go through a list of basic vocabulary that the child would have met in his reading books — the, in, at, am on, up, and, go, look, come, here, this, me he, we, mother, father, car, for. Continue for ten minutes or until the child's writing vocabulary is exhausted. Very able children need little prompting but sometimes it is necessary to suggest a category of words.

'Do you know how to write your number words like the word one?
'Do you know how to write your colour words like the word red?
'Do you know how to write your days of the week like the word Monday?
'Do you know how to write your months of the year like the word May?
'Do you know how to write any other names of children like Bill, Peter?'

Scoring

Each word completed accurately is marked as correct. If the child accidentally writes a word that is correct but reads it as another word or does not know what it is that word is scored an error. Words written in mirror image are scored as correct only if the child actually wrote them in the correct sequence. Groups of words such as look, looks, looked, looking, and sat, fat, mat, hat, are allowed as separate words.

Attainment

Some children can not produce their own names. Half of the children in Robinson's study (1973) aged 5:6 could not write more than four to seven words. Only four children at this age wrote more than 13 words. The results for children aged 6:0 were far higher, the mean score for two samples being 26 and 29. Even with the ten-minute time limit the writing vocabulary of able children was by no means exhausted. One child wrote 79 words in ten minutes.

A developmental record of a child's progress may be kept by taking an inventory of writing vocabulary at several points in time — at entry, after six months and after one year. In the examples for Ross, Nicola and Joanne the progress of each child is evident even though they are at three different levels of attainment.

Stanine scores for one group of children are provided.

Research Group	Writing Vocabulary (Normalized Scores — Stanine Groups)									
282 urban children aged 6:0-7:3 in 1978	**Stanine group**	1	2	3	4	5	6	7	8	9
	Test score	0-13	14-19	20-28	29-35	36-45	46-55	56-70	71-80	81-

Reliability: 34 urban children aged 5:6 in 1972, (Robinson) 0.97, test-retest.
Validity: Correlation with reading; 50 urban children aged 5:6 in 1972, (Robinson) 0.82.

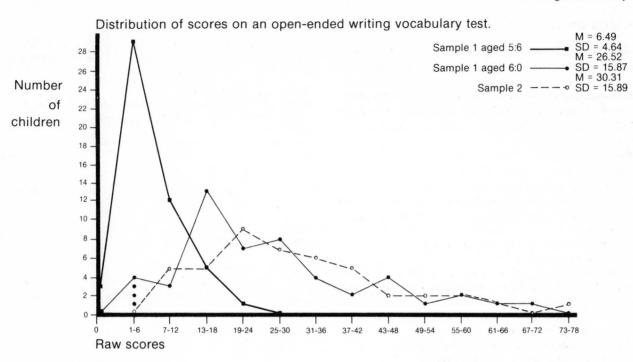

Distribution of scores on an open-ended writing vocabulary test.

Sample 1 aged 5:6 M = 6.49 SD = 4.64
Sample 1 aged 6:0 M = 26.52 SD = 15.87
Sample 2 M = 30.31 SD = 15.89

Number of children

Raw scores

A dictation test

Simple sentences are used as a dictation test. The child is given credit for every *sound* that he writes correctly, even though the word may not be correct. The scores give some indication of the child's ability to analyse the word he hears or says and to find some way of recording the sounds he hears as letters.

Administration

Say to the child:
'I am going to read you a story.
When I have read it through once I will read it again very slowly so that you can write down the words in the story.'
Read the test sentences at normal speed:
'Some of the words are hard.
Say them slowly and think how you would write them.'
Dictate slowly. When the child comes to a problem word, say:
'You say it slowly. How would you start to write it . . .
What else can you hear.'
If the child cannot complete the word say:
'We'll leave that word. The next one is . . .'
Point to where to write the next word if this helps the child.

There are five alternative dictation tests with one or two sentences. When retesting it is advisable to use an alternate form. The tests are listed on the following page.

Recording

Write the text below the child's version.

$\dfrac{\text{hm}}{\text{him}}$	$\dfrac{\text{skol}}{\text{school}}$	$\dfrac{\text{b}}{\text{big}}$

Tests and scoring*

Score 1 point for each *sound* (phoneme) the child has analysed that is numbered 1 to 37 below and total out of 37.

Changes in letter order
Where the child has made a change in letter order, take 1 mark off for that word. For example

$$\frac{\text{ma}}{\text{am}} \quad 2 - 1 = 1 \qquad \frac{\text{gonig}}{\text{going}} \quad 5 - 1 = 4$$

Alternatives accepted
Alternatives are accepted when the *sound* analysis is a useful one. For example

$$\frac{\text{skool}}{\text{school}} \qquad \frac{\text{tace}}{\text{take}}$$

Additions and omissions
1 If a letter does not have a number underneath it, it receives *no* score, even if a preceding letter is omitted. For example

$$\frac{\text{tody}}{\text{today}} = 3$$

2 Additions do not affect scoring as long as numbered letters are included. For example

$$\frac{\text{todae}}{\text{today}} = 4$$

Make some notes about

- any sequencing errors
- omission of sounds
- unusual use of space on the page
- unusual placement of letters within words.

These may provide teaching points later in the child's programme.

*Susan Robinson and Barbara Watson devised and used these tests in the reading recovery programme, where they proved to be useful indicators of the child's ability to go from his analysis of sounds in spoken words to written forms for representing these sounds. In that sense this is not a true dictation or spelling test.

Administration and scoring

Select one of the following alternate Forms; A, B, C, D or E.

Form A

I   have   a   big   dog   at   home.
1   2 3 4   5   6 7 8   9 10 11   12 13   14 15 16

T o d a y   I   a m   g o i n g   to   t a k e   h i m
17 18 19 20   21 22   23 24 25 26 27   28 29 30   31 32 33

t o   s c h oo l .
34 35   36 37

Form B

M u m   h a s   g o n e   u p   t o   t̲h̲e   s̲h̲o p .
1 2 3   4 5 6   7 8 9   10 11   12 13   14 15   16 17 18

S̲h̲e   w i l l   g e t   m i l k   a n d
19 20   21 22 23   24 25 26   27 28 29 30   31 32 33

b r e a d .
34 35 36   37

Form C

I   c a n   s e e   t̲h̲e   r e d
1   2 3 4   5 6   7 8   9 10 11

b o a t   t̲h̲a t   w e   a r e   g o i n g
12 13 14   15 16 17   18 19   20 21   22 23 24 25 26

t o   h a v e   a   r i d e   i n .
27 28   29 30 31   32   33 34 35   36 37

Form D

T̲h̲e   b u s   i s   c o m i n g .   I t
1 2   3 4 5   6 7   8 9 10 11 12 13   14 15

w i l l   s t o p   h e r e   t o   l e t   m e
16 17 18   19 20 21 22   23 24 25   26 27   28 29 30   31 32

g e t   o n .
33 34 35   36 37

Form E

T̲h̲e   b o̲y̲   i s   r i d i n g   h i s   b i k e .
1 2   3 4   5 6   7 8 9 10 11 12   13 14 15   16 17 18

H e   c a n   g o   v e r y   f a s t   o n   i t .
19 20   21 22 23   24 25   26 27 28 29   30 31 32 33   34 35   36 37

Research Group	Dictation Test (Normalized scores — Stanine Groups)									
280 urban children aged 6:0 - 7:3 in 1978	**Stanine group**	1	2	3	4	5	6	7	8	9
	Test score	0-3	4-9	10-17	18-27	28-31	32-35	36-37	—	—

Writing a story

An older child who can write 50 or more words is too competent for the Writing Vocabulary Test. He should be encouraged to write a story of several sentences or paragraphs (with as little help as possible) to provide a basis for grouping children's stories from say A to E. An earlier record for one child can be compared with a later one to estimate progress.

Spelling

Older children can be given a spelling test. The useful information on these tests is the evidence that the correct responses provide of strengths (words known, strategies that work — first letters sounded and so on) and the evidence that the incorrect responses provide of gaps, confusions or interfering strategies. The test score or spelling-age is information of lesser value. Some sources would be

- Arvidson Spelling List —NZCER
- Schonell Spelling Test
- NZCER Basic Word List.

Summarizing the Diagnostic Survey Results

The Diagnostic Summary brings all the test results together. It describes the child's strengths and weaknesses, and indicates the strategies that are used and those that are not used.

From the detailed information which the survey yields it has proved useful to summarize the results under the headings listed on the Diagnostic Survey Summary Sheet (page 95).

Book reading
Analysis of errors to show what cues the child uses.

Test results
Analysis of strategies used by the child.
  Useful strategies on text.
  Problem strategies on text.
  Useful strategies with words.
  Problem strategies with words.
  Useful strategies with letters and sounds.
  Problem strategies with letters and sounds.

Looking for Strategies

There are several reasons for this approach to summarizing the Survey.

• Language is organized hierarchically on several levels. Three have been selected here — letter, word, and text (a general term to stand for phrase, sentence or larger text).
• It has been argued that although the reader has stored items of knowledge he also needs to use strategies for operating on these stores (see Paul, below, for an example of a boy with weak item-using strategies) and for relating one store of information to another.

Good observation rather than modern linguistic theory led a talented reading clinician Grace Fernald in 1943 to formulate statements about the relationships of letters, words and texts in reading.

'Groups of words must be the focus of attention in reading. Attending to the words as separate units, as in word-by-word reading loses important meanings. The meaning of a word can vary with the group in which it occurs or, in another way, a group of words has a certain meaning.

The sentence is the context in which the *meaning of the word group* is confirmed.

The known word is the unit at which level the precision of the word group is usually confirmed.

For the unknown, unfamiliar, forgotten or misperceived word the reader's attention must go to clusters of letters or even to individual letters but whether these are right or not must be confirmed at the level of the word unit.'

She insisted therefore that in writing the word should always be written as a unit, and in reading words should always be used in context.

The way of summarizing the survey results adopted in the summary sheet is deficient in that it does not allow for the description and detection of strengths and weaknesses in those strategies which relate one level of linguistic organization to another. We do not yet know much about such strategies.

Some examples of what is meant by reading strategies are given in case reports for:

• Mary at 6:0 — Early Reading.
• Paul at 6:9 — First Reading Books.
• Brian at 7:3 — Use of Graded Paragraphs.

Other examples are given in the report of a class survey and a research study reporting reading recovery procedures (pages 35 and 67).

The questions listed in the next section helped some teachers to describe the reading strategies that young children use.

Useful Strategies on Text

Look at the Running Record of book reading where the child is performing adequately (90 to 100 percent accuracy) and try to find some evidence of how effectively he works with the sequences of cues. Also look at Concepts About Print Test items. Use these questions as a guide to your analysis of the records.

Location and movement

Does he control directional movement?
— left to right?
— top to bottom?
— return sweep?
Does he locate particular cues in print? Which cues?
Does he read word by word?

Language

Does he control language well?
Does he read for meaning?
Does he control book language?
Does he have a good memory for text?
Does he read for the precise message?

Behaviour at difficulties

Does he seek help?
Does he try again?
Does he search for further cues? How?
Note unusual behaviours.

Substitutions

Do the substitutions the child uses make sense? (Meaning)
Do they make an acceptable sentence in English? (Structure)
Could they occur in grammar?
Are some of the letters the same? (Visual or graphic cues)

Self-correction

Does he return to the beginning of the line?
Does he return back a few words?
Does he repeat the word only?
Does he read on to the end of the line?
Does he repeat only the initial sound of a word?
Note unusual behaviour.

Cross-checking strategies

Language and movement, one to one matching.
Language and visual cues.
Language, one to one matching and visual cues.
Does he ignore discrepancies?

Useful Strategies on Words

Check Concepts About Print (CAP), Text reading, Writing Vocabulary, Dictation Test, and Word tests.

The visual features of words

On CAP recognizes line rearrangement.
On CAP recognizes word rearrangement.
On CAP recognizes that the first and last letters are rearranged.
On CAP recognizes that the medial letters are rearranged.

On text can attend to detail.
Responds to initial letters.
Responds to initial and final letters.
Relates to some prior visual or writing experience of that word.

The sounds of words

Can order words in a cut-up sentence.
Can articulate words slowly.
Can break up words into sounds (as in a dictated sentence).

Useful Strategies on Letters

Check Concepts About Print, Text reading, Letter Identification, Writing Vocabulary, Dictation Test and Word tests.

Movement

Does the child form (write) some letters easily?
Does he form many letters without a copy?

Visual

Which letters can he identify?
How does he identify them?
Which letters does he use as cues in reading?
Could he detect an error because of a mismatch of letters?
(Which letters were difficult?)
(Which letters were confused one with another?)

Sounds

How does a child attempt a word in the Dictation Test?
Does he articulate it slowly?
Can he isolate the first sound of a word that he hears?
Can he give other words that start with the same sound?

Case Summaries

Mary aged 6:0

Initial testing: 4.5.77
Initial status: Early reading — Caption Books.

1   Book reading
Mary read three Caption Books: *I am big* (seen), *The Bear Family* (seen) and *I am little* (unseen) with 94, 87, 75 percent accuracy and 0:3, 1:5, 0:8 self-correction rates. She read half of a red level supplementary, *Wake Up* (Star 1₃) which was not scored.

2   Test results
Mary's score on Letter Identification was 34/54, on Concepts About Print was 13/24, on the Word tests was 3/15 and 0/30, on Writing Vocabulary was 2 and on the Dictation Test was 8/37.

3   Useful strategies on text
Mary uses fluent book language.
She moves across the print from left to right with return sweep.

Problem strategies on text
Mary's fluent language response overrides visual and locating cues.
Under the tester's monitoring she *can* locate word by word and *can* attend the words she knows in print *(I, am, is, here)*, but independently her language response is too fluent to allow any integration of cues.
Her self-correction rates are almost nil.
She does not attend to letter cues. Her miscues had zero graphic correspondence.

4   Useful strategies on words
Mary recognized *I, here, am* in isolation.
She wrote

I	si	a	May
	am		Mary

She analysed some initial sounds (have, big, home) on the dictation test.

Problem strategies on words
Mary does not attend to words while reading unless asked to 'Look carefully and read with your finger.' Locating in print and coordinating finger and speech in word-by-word reading is a difficult coordination for her to make.

5   Useful strategies on letters
Mary identified 34/54 letters by name.
She knows some sound-to-letter relationships.

Problem strategies on letters
Mary confuses 15 letters:

I	F	I	j	q	g	i	r	b	h	k	j	b	b	O
L	E	T	f	u	y	l	q	d	n	x	i	p	g	Q

Diagnostic summary
Mary has made some progress in the visual area in isolation but her fluent language overrides visual cues and prevents word-by-word reading. Discrepancies don't signal to her to recheck and self-correct.

Paul aged 6:9

Initial testing: 9.8.77
Initial status: First Readers

1   Book reading
Paul read *Early in the Morning* Red 1 Level (seen) with 98 percent accuracy and 0:1 self-corrections and *The Lazy Pig* (PM lj) with 79 percent accuracy and 1:3 self-corrections.

2   Test results
Paul's score on Letter Identification was 31/54, on Concepts About Print was 19/24, on the Word tests was 3/15 and 4/30, on Writing Vocabulary was 7 and on the Dictation Test was 11/37.

3   Useful strategies on text
Paul predicts meaningful language from picture clues with 1:1 matching, using some initial letter-to-sound knowledge. He self-corrects some mismatches and known words.

Problem strategies on text
His miscues have semantic and syntactic acceptability but not graphic acceptability. He is very distractable and often uses diversionary tactics to escape the reading task.

4   Useful strategies on words
He identified 3/15, and 4/30 words in isolation.
He wrote 7 words.
He uses word knowledge in reading text.
He analyses some sounds within words.

Problem strategies on words
Recall of words, especially basic words, seems to be a difficult area.
Language overrides word knowledge in reading.

awake		woke
up	(5 x)	am

5   Useful strategies on letters
He identified 31/54 letter symbols by letter name.
He analyses initial sounds and some sounds within words.
He uses some initial letter-to-sound knowledge in reading.

Problem strategies on letters

He confused $\frac{n}{u}\ \frac{u}{y}\ \frac{x}{z}\ \frac{z}{x}\ \frac{E}{F}$ on Letter Identi-

fication and $\frac{W}{M}$ in writing.

Diagnostic summary

Paul has shown progress in component skills of reading but his age and habituated diversionary tactics, his difficulty in recalling sight words and his overriding language response in reading text have prevented any rapid reading progress.

An analysis of error behaviour: Brian

The graded paragraphs of the Neale Analysis of Reading Ability (Form B) were administered to Brian, a boy aged 7:3 with very good reading strategies in his third year of instruction. In addition to standard scoring of the test this running record of reading behaviour was made by a second year Education student without training or experience in teaching. For the text of the paragraphs the reader is referred to Neale (1958).

Paragraph one (p.17)

√ √ √ √ √ √
√ √ √ √ √ √
√ √ √ √ √ √ √ √
√ √ √ √ √ √

Running words	:	26
Accuracy	:	100%
Error rate	:	Nil
Self-correction rate	:	Nil
Repetition	:	Nil
Prompts	:	Nil
Comprehension	:	100%

Paragraph two (p.19)

√ √ √ √ √
√ √ √ √ √
√ √ $\frac{h}{had}$|had $\;$ √ √ √
√ √ √ $\frac{n}{not}$|not √ √
√ √ √ √ √ √
√ √ √ √ √ √
√ √ √ √ $\frac{√}{held}$ $\frac{h}{held}$|held √
√ √ √ the |R |SC √ √ √
√ √ √ √

Running words	:	49
Accuracy	:	100%
Error rate	:	Nil
Self-correction rate	:	(One)
Repetition	:	Nil
Prompts	:	Nil
Comprehension	:	50%
Solving strategies	:	First letter sounding (h, n)

Paragraph three (p.21)

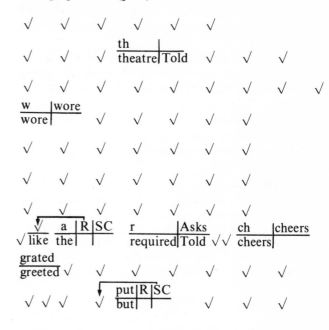

Running words	:	72
Accuracy	:	96%
Error rate	:	1 in 24
Self-correction rate	:	2 in 7
Repetition	:	Nil
Prompts	:	theatre, required
Comprehension	:	25%
Solving strategies	:	First sound (th, ch, r, w). Beginning and end (greeted, but). Syntax and meaning both in error (put, but). Syntax acceptable, meaning not (grated). Letter cues (a/the).

Paragraph four (p.23)

√ √ √ √ $\dfrac{m}{mournful} \Big| \dfrac{}{Asks} Told$ √ √

√ √ √ $\dfrac{distant}{deserted}$ $\dfrac{cast-lay}{castle}$

√ $\dfrac{cased}{ceased}$ √ $\dfrac{ab}{abruptly} \Big| \dfrac{am}{} \Big| \dfrac{amb}{} \Big| \dfrac{ambrutli}{}$ √

√ √ √ √ √

√ √ √ $\dfrac{never\ the\ less}{nevertheless}$ √ $\dfrac{pro}{proceeded} \Big| \dfrac{}{Asks} Told$

$\dfrac{c}{cautiously} \Big| Told$ √ √ √ √ √ $\dfrac{mysteries}{mysterious}$ √

$\dfrac{cowrige}{courage}$ and with $\Big|$ SC $\dfrac{mountining}{mounting}$

$\dfrac{C}{curiosity} \Big| Told$ √ √ √ √ √ √

√ $\dfrac{sce\ ali}{scarcely}$ $\dfrac{dare}{daring} \Big|$ SC √ √ √ √

√ √ √ √ √ √

√ √ √ $\dfrac{the}{their}$ √

√ √ √ √ √ √ $\dfrac{e}{exhausted} \Big| Told$

√ √ √ √ √ √ √ $\dfrac{im}{imprisoned} \Big| \dfrac{}{Asks} Told$

√ √ √ √ √ √ √ √ √

Running words   : 92
Accuracy   : 82.6%
Error rate   : 1 in 5
Self-correction rate : 1 in 9
Repetition   : Nil
Prompting   : mournful, proceeded
                       exhausted, imprisoned
                       cautiously, curiosity
Comprehension   : 80%

Scoring and analysis

This is provided in the table on page 34.

Descriptive comments

Brian read word by word, staccato, at a fast pace. He ignored punctuation and paused at difficult words and the end of lines, losing meaning and sense. Intonation was flat and even with little variation.

In correcting himself Brian went back to the previous word but not to the beginning of the sentence or line.

Brian used initial letters or clusters and last letters or clusters for cues. He did not use medial sounds, syllables or clusters as efficiently.

Recommendations

Although only 7 years of age Brian has a reading age of 9 years and this analysis of his reading of continuous text shows that two emphases typical of 9-year-old learning are required in Brian's programme. He could now develop a more consciously controlled syllabic attack, with attention to medial vowels and syllables. Meantime he should place more value on meaning by using punctuation cues, by phrasing, and by searching until the difficult word makes sense.

This may mean a temporary drop in fluency while syllabic attack and semantic checks are incorporated into his present patterns of reading behaviour.*

* The author is indebted to the careful observation of Mrs M. O'Rourke for this case study.

From a Running Record of a Seven-Year-Old Using Tests from the Neale Analysis of Reading

Paragraph	One	Two	Three	Four
Running words	26	49	72	92
Accuracy	100%	100%	96%	83%
Error rate	nil	nil	1:24	1:5
Self-correction rate	nil	(one)	1:3	1:9
Repetition	nil	nil	nil	nil
Prompts	nil	nil	theatre, required	mourning proceeded exhausted imprisoned cautiously curiosity
Comprehension	100%	50%	25%	80%
Solving strategies	nil	first letters sounded (h,n)	**1** first sound (th, ch, r, w) **2** beginning & end (greeted, but) **3** syntax + meaning both in error (put, but) **4** syntax acceptable, meaning not (grated) **5** letter cues (a/the)	**1** syllabic attack (nevertheless, in-, ab-, pro-, dar-) **2** first letter attack always correct **3** beginning and end correct (ceased, mounting, mysterious, courage, scarcely) **4** syntax + meaning + letter cues (deserted, d-s-t) **5** syntax + letter cues but not meaning (cased)

A Survey of Infant School Reading

To demonstrate that this survey can discriminate between groups of children in classrooms where they are at different stages of reading progress, the results in the table below from a city school are reported.

On the right-hand side are the results from a frequently used word recognition test, the Schonell R₁. The mean scores do not discriminate well between children until they have completed the twelve Little Books and the scores do not indicate what the failing children need to learn.

In the first three columns are scores for the Concepts About Print, Letter Identification and *Ready to Read* Word Test. Note that the first two tests can be administered to the youngest groups before the Word Test becomes useful. Note also that in this particular school two high progress groups of young entrants were already as competent on the Concepts About Print Test as two slow groups of second year children on books Green 2 and Green 3, *Ready to Read*.

A Survey of Infant School Reading									
Reading Group	Number in Group	Concepts About Print		Letter Identification		Ready to Read Word Test		Schonell R1	
		Mean Score	Stanine score (1968)	Mean score	Stanine score (1968)	Mean score	Stanine score (1968)	Mean score	Stanine score (1968)
New entrants	9	8.0	4	8.0	4	0.8	1-2	0	0
Caption books	11	9.2	4	11.9	4	1.6	3	0	0
Price Milburn 1a	8	12.2	5	20.0	4	2.1	4	1.2	4
McKee *Tip*	4	13.3	4	21.3	4	6.5	5	1.2	4
Ready to Read: Blue 2	6	14.8	5	31.8	5	7.5	5	3.8	5
Ready to Read: Green 2	9	12.5	5	37.7	5	13.0	6	(No data)	(No data)
Ready to Read: Green 3	7	13.5	5	39	5	14.0	6	7.4	6
Ready to Read: The Hungry Lambs	9	15.3	6	48	6	14.0	6	10.9	6

Organizing to Prevent Reading Failure

The organization of instruction to prevent reading failure requires the attention of teachers and administrators. Overseas research has shown that a critical factor relating to the level of progress is not the method, nor the materials, but the quality of the teaching.

I hope to point to ways in which better organization in schools can improve the quality of the teaching of reading at a time when the foundations of all future interactions with written language are being laid.

A particular challenge is presented to New Zealanders because we take children into school at their fifth birthday. As no other country does this, we have no models to follow. Programmes from Britain or America will not give us a guide as to how we might organize for this particular feature of our education which forces us to individualize our instruction in a way that is different from other countries.

What happens to the 5-year-olds who come into school? How are they grouped? When are they moved to another group? or to a new class? What exactly happens about shifting groups of children from one class to another? Each school knows what it does, but there is no description of what everyone else does and no evaluation of one practice against another. It would be interesting to compare schools, noting differences in organization and differences in the criteria used for moving children. We would find different solutions in schools of different sizes. The growth rate in a district would make a difference because if one school has new entrants coming at the rate of a whole new class a month it is going to have different kinds of problems and different solutions for class organization from a school where one class fills up in the first six months or in the first year. These questions are related to the quality of instruction given to the new entrants.

Countries decide on some arbitrary basis, for historical reasons, or custom, or convention, the age at which children start school. Once the large group of children is in a classroom then their lives will be different from what they would have been had they not come into formal education at that time. Simply bringing them into formal education, into a reception class, into developmental programmes changes the life opportunities for those children. Whatever the child has been able to learn up till the point where he comes to school, whatever his behaviours are, whatever his response to his environment has been, it now goes through some transitions. The teacher in the reception class is trying to bring the children from those varied behaviours that they learned in their preschool years towards some behaviours shared with other children. The teacher is trying to encourage a transition from the behaviour that the child brings to school to some behaviour he can use in school on academic tasks. He may have limited language patterns and these have to be brought to something that can be worked on along with other children in a programme. He may be withdrawn, and his social behaviour may be brought to the point where he can work with a group.

Because we invite children into formal education we must give up the idea that 'they ripen and mature so that after a while they begin to read'. This is not true. Teachers and schools are engineering certain transitions. I think this concept is very important. It gets us away from the idea of the reception class teacher as one who is just minding the children until they mature, at which point they can be moved on to a teacher who is really going to do some work with them. That is far from the true situation. If we look at the changes made by children in the reception class these transitions seem even more important than those made later in primary school. If teachers monitored these transitions sensitively and individualized their teaching for the slow-to-learn pupils as a result of those observations, they would be improving the quality of their teaching.

The entry class is a most important class. Where do the reception class teachers learn their trade? How much help did they have when they first began teaching new entrants? I suspect they depend upon the Senior Teacher of Junior Classes. One of my pleas would be that we organize for someone with experience to take the new entrants and if, as must occur, new teachers present themselves for this task, then they need initial and continuing training for a period. As far as the children are concerned, this beginning is a very, very important time.

In 1964 I watched children's progress through the first year of school by taking records at weekly intervals of what they were doing and what they were saying. To give two examples of the long-term outcomes of their progress, one of the boys who went along fairly slowly for the first six months ended up with marks in the 90's for six subjects in School Certificate year. Another boy at the same school got into a terrible tangle in the first year, had severe reading problems, went to a reading clinic for several years and finally passed School Certificate. That was a success story for a child whose whole schooling has been a trouble to him because of the inappropriate learning that he did in the first year at school. At the end of this study I was saying that we ought to reduce our new entrant classes; we ought not to let them rise above 25 children. This seemed to be the impossible dream at that time but now I am more hopeful that in this very important first year we could reduce classes to not more than 20 or 25. The purpose of this is to individualize the instruction and to ensure that children move into reading without confusions.

We have children entering school throughout the year, and we recognize that children become ready for book reading at different rates, some within a month or two months of entry to school, the average children not until 5:6 and some children not until the end of the first year. There is considerable variation in the rate at which New Zealand children move into simple graded material. In my opinion, the explanation for these delays, is not that the child is taking a year to mature but that he is taking a year to learn the early reading behaviours that are the foundation of later success when he is introduced to simple graded texts. The children have these behaviours when they enter school, some take about six months to learn them, some take at least a year. We can pick up some children at 6 years who have not acquired effective control of these early reading behaviours.

Here I want to add a critical note. We have individualized the rate at which we introduce children to programmes, but I don't believe we have paid sufficient attention to individualizing the tasks and instruction that we provide during that period. It is not only that these children are moving at different rates; some of them need more help with some aspects of the task than others.

To be able to detect these needs we will have to observe a little more closely than we have in the past, what the 5-year-old is doing and what he is capable of. Some of my work has been directed towards providing teachers with some structured situations in which they can improve their observation of children's actual behaviour to record with greater accuracy what they can do, and by implication, what they cannot do.

If there is no magical moment at which a child is 'ready' what can we look for in the first year that indicates progress? I look for movement or change in the child's behaviour. My criteria for progress during the first year would be that he moves from those responses he can give when he comes to school toward some other goals that I see as appropriate for him. I am looking for *movement in appropriate directions*. And only careful monitoring will assure me that the child is not practising inappropriate behaviours. For if I do not watch what he is doing, and if I do not capture what is happening in records of some kind, Johnny, who never gets under my feet and who never comes really into a situation where I can truly see what he is doing, may, in fact, for six months or even a year, practise behaviours that will handicap him in reading.

One of the critical areas is directional behaviour. The boy who had some difficulty in getting School Certificate was a boy who was quite confused about direction. At the end of the first year he would happily go from right to left as often as he would to from left to right. Visual learning in reading is nonsense if you don't happen to be looking at the print in the appropriate direction. This is what had happened to him. Organizing for preventing reading failure depends a great deal on providing opportunities for observing just what children are doing.

I would like to expand on this idea of observing. My emphasis on this came from my work as a researcher rather than from my work as a teacher. I decided that because the explanations in books did not seem to account for my successes with remedial clients I would pretend that I knew nothing about what reading is and what we should do in reading. I would adopt a neutral stance and observe exactly what children did. In taking this position I stepped out of a teaching role entirely and became much more like a scientist setting up a situation and recording precisely what happens.

When I write of observing children closely this is what I mean! There must be times when the teacher stops teaching and becomes an observer, a time when she must drop all her pre-suppositions about what this child is like, and when she listens very carefully and records very precisely what the child can in fact do.

One must organize for such observation times. In this situation it is difficult not to prompt, to help, to teach, to question. These activities do not have any place in the observation situation which is a completely different thing. To prevent reading failure teachers must have time to observe what children are able to do. This means time out from teaching, time set aside for observing. The younger the child and the poorer the reader, the more time the teacher requires for observing and for thinking about what she observes.

Knowing the pressures on teachers one has to be realistic about this. What would be the most economical time from the teachers' point of view to carry out thorough observation checks to catch up the children who are either confused or not making progress? I hope the class teacher would observe her children as often as possible, from week to week perhaps. But drastic changes occur in children's lives. Children change school, children change classes, they lose parents who leave the home, they have intermittent absences for legitimate health reasons. It is not sufficient to leave the decision to observe or not to the class teacher. When our fifth birthday entrants turn 6 years of age somebody in the school should be responsible for checking on reading behaviour.

Why do I recommend this at the end of the child's first year? It allows the checking process to go on all year, for it would be impossible to carry out this type of check on all children at the one time, say, at the end of a year. The child is given sufficient time to adjust to the school situation. The child who is slow to begin can be given a variety of opportunities to make progress. The teacher who finds that a certain focus within the programme does not suit the child can emphasize a different aspect. The sixth birthday check maximizes the opportunities, minimizes the pressure on the child, does not leave the child for more than one year to practise bad habits that might handicap him and be very hard to unlearn. If you leave it until some of the children are 6:6 you have shortened the time for remedial help before the question of Standard One promotion comes up. The longer we leave them, the shorter time we have, and the more they have practised inappropriate responding.

The 6-year-old check does call for organizing. The ST(JC) must, in the first instance, be allocated time for this task, to establish the programme in her school, but the ST(JC) can then introduce her staff to the 6-year-old checks. We must organize for this sixth birthday check. When we have applied the 6-year-old check, obviously, we will need some very skilful teachers to teach children who have been defined by the observation procedures as children with special needs. Inexperienced teachers are little help to slow children, or to children with difficulties who are slow, or to children with difficulties who are reading their first books. The children with special needs will be hard to teach. The teacher needs experience with a wide variety of approaches, and the ingenuity and flexibility to do different things with different children. Within a school this calls for organizing so that you can have these kind of people available for the children sorted out by the 6-year-old check.

These skilful teachers should be given recognition for the kind of job they are able to do. The task may not be very rewarding. It is not quite as exciting as taking a high progress group. It is a job that carries more strain, and one's pupils will, inevitably, have lower achievement than those of other teachers at the end of the year. The school has to recognize that this person is a very important person and needs appropriate rewards for tackling this task. The response of these children will not be rapid, even when you give them a highly skilled and experienced teacher, who uses special techniques. Only some of them will make a spurt in that second year and 'catch up'. The children who do this will be the children who haven't really taken much notice of the programme in the first year and who now begin to take notice and to take off. In my studies there were only one or two such children. Most children who had made little progress by 6 years are children who brought some limitation or handicap to school, who are going to carry that handicap with them and who are going to have to learn to read in spite of it.

What can one look for in early reading in order to prevent failure? Let me make an analogy with mathematics and the changes we have seen there in the last few years. Almost nobody now thinking about the young child moving into learning maths is going to think in terms of how many arithmetical items he knows. Almost everybody will be thinking 'what mathematical operations can he carry out'! Although we may not yet have definitive descriptions of the strategies or operations used or to be acquired in early reading this is the kind of shift in our thinking we have to make. In order to prevent early reading failure *we should be looking for strategies the child is using*. We have to observe him reading book material as well as checking on his word recognition. You can hear a child correcting himself as he reads. As he is reading along, he stops, he goes back. Nobody suggested that he should do this. This is a strategy that tells me he is monitoring his own reading. If he is listening to what he is saying he has recognized that something doesn't fit, goes back, and he takes responsibility for working on it.

This does relate to organizing for reading. The high progress readers move into reading, they get certain help and then by the time they are about 6 years of age, they are monitoring their own reading in helpful ways. If they are given material of an appropriate level they have some strategies which will help them to teach themselves from that material.

The child who is not able to do this monitoring of his own reading is the one who needs the teacher. Observation records of teachers show that they allow good readers to read much more than they do slow readers. There are reasons why this occurs. The slow child takes longer to read, and he is reading much more limited text. The high progress reader is reading involved text and takes several pages to get through an important part of the story. If there is anything in this about organizing, it suggests that if we simply manipulate twice as much time for the slow children as for the good readers we might in fact be doing quite a lot for the prevention of reading failure.

So it is important to look for strategies, to look for progress in the child's reading strategies, and particularly to see that children are getting to the point where they in fact can tutor themselves. Situations must be set up where they can carry on without much attention from the teacher. This leaves her more time to work with slow progress readers.

A major problem in thinking about what school organization will improve the quality of instruction, is the individual learner versus the group instruction dilemma. Formal education procedures are, of necessity, group procedures, but the best progress for a particular child will result from individual instruction. Our compromise between the large class procedure and the individual one is to group children. This is our dilemma; to individualize instruction as much as possible, even under group procedures. One cannot justify teaching all children on the assumption that all need the same kind of teaching. Teachers do recognize the great differences between children, and within children, and in their background experiences and personality traits.

The need for organizing reading instruction in order to provide in an adequate way for individual differences is recognized but much still remains to be done in practical application. This implies different programmes for different children, not just different rates.

There is a strong emphasis on individual tuition in the present system in Sweden. One of the main regulations of the Swedish Education Acts of 1962 and 1969 is that the personal resources of the individual child must not only be respected but must be the starting point for the planning of education and teaching. According to objectives stated in the school law the school must simulate the child's personal growth towards his development as a free, self-active, self-confident, harmonious human being. The school *must* give individual education.

Some steps taken in Sweden to further a diagnostic approach and the individualization of the teaching of reading are these:

• Class size has been reduced to a maximum of 25 in the first three years — but the average size for the country as a whole for the first three years lies between 17 and 18 children per class.

• Better opportunities than before are provided for individual tutoring, small group teaching, teaching in clinics and the provision of special classes of various kinds.

• In the first three grades, there is now written into the teaching load of each teacher, a weekly two-hour block of time for tutoring any individual child in his class who, in his judgment, needs such help. Obviously there has to be organization for this when it is part of the teacher's weekly work.

• Another procedure has contributed significantly to the individualization of teaching. In the first grade, for example, one half of the class meets with the teacher for the first two hours of the day. The second half comes to school two hours late and stays two hours later on. This kind of staggering might be organized for if there was extra help around. This is an interesting way of reducing numbers and getting more individual instruction for children having particular difficulties.

To prevent reading disabilities, observation of children's progress, and individualization of teaching are stressed.

In summary

To help those children who are becoming reading cripples in the first year of schooling, we do have to organize:

• For using strengths of teaching staffs at appropriate points.

• For new teaching staff to have opportunities to gain these strengths by observing people who are expert in working with them.

• For opportunities to see precisely where a child is, what strategies he is employing.

• For picking up those children who are employing strategies which are going to be an impediment to their progress.

• To give more reading time to those children who are making slow progress.

• For individual teaching.

I think the time is ripe for innovation and a sharing of ideas on how we can better organize effectively for individualization of instruction for the slower learners in the first year of school.

The AIMS/ETC of Reading Recovery

A remedial programme for any particular child (or for a group) should be based on observation of what the child can and does do at the time of the survey. The following principles should be considered in the organizing of programmes of re-teaching.

Acceleration

The child requiring remedial tuition is already retarded or making very slow progress. He must make up for lost time. Both the scheduling of lessons and the choice of learning activity must be arranged in such a way that no further slowing up takes place. The lessons must be regular and frequent. The child must be highly motivated. Unless it is absolutely essential, the child should not be diverted from print to pictorial material and puzzles, as these are not directly related to the progress he needs to make. Similarly, a long-term diversion to teach him the sound equivalents of letters, using isolated words, may retard his reading progress further if reading is thought to be performance on a continuous text. He must learn such details, but related to his book-reading lessons.

The principle of acceleration in the remedial programme is not an easy one to implement and must be constantly borne in mind.

Intensive Programme

The best remedial tuition will be given in short lessons under the close supervision of one teacher preferably every day, or even twice a day. (Twice-a-week sessions for groups of children are a weak approach to meeting learning needs.) Only a small amount of new material should be introduced at each lesson, and many, many practice sessions are required. The child who does not know when his attempts are good and when they are poor must be reinforced by a teacher immediately he makes an appropriate response. The teacher's close supervision will also allow her to detect when some interfering or handicapping type of response (from old habits or newly-learned) creeps in, and to swiftly arrange for a better response to occur. She may structure the task, (e.g. provide a masking card or a pointer) or she may need to teach some new basis for making choices among words.

One teacher per pupil is the only practical method of working with children who have extreme difficulty in learning to read. If group teaching is all that can be offered to groups of children who are not severely retarded, the principles of an intensive programme such as close supervision of the child's responding and short lessons held often, are still vitally important.

Minutiae — Getting Down to Detail

In learning to read, the child making normal progress picks up and organizes for himself a wealth of detailed information about letters, print, words and reading, with a spontaneity that leads teachers to believe that many of these things do not need to be taught. But, for the failing child, it is necessary to check for knowledge of the simplest details and to teach specifically the letter distinctions, the different features of capital and lower-case letters, of print and written scripts, of slight differences between words, or some basic list of words, or letter-sound correspondences, and phoneme blends, and how to read punctuation, etc.

However, when the teacher becomes involved in minutiae the principle of acceleration is threatened. The child cannot afford to spend time in detail that he already knows. Tuition must be a gap-filling or a confusion clearing type of activity. It should be a detour from a programme which is really focussed on reading books, a detour taken for attention to some particular aspect of detail in print, in the clear realization that knowledge of the detail will be of limited value unless it can be used on the run in reading continuous text. Minutiae or details should be supplementary to the main programme. But they must receive attention.

Sequence

Every school and classroom has some teaching sequence by which reading is presented to children. For the child who has become a reading failure in that setting it will probably not be sufficient to change to a different teacher, different material and a different approach to instruction.

Failing children are far more different among themselves than average children. They are a heterogeneous group whose strengths and weaknesses are different and whose learning tangles may need quite different 'untangling' techniques.

Programmes and teaching sequences of any standard kind are unlikely to meet the needs of severely retarded readers. While the commercial kit used with a group of slow readers may be a slight improvement on nothing, the ideal programme should be individually tailored to a particular child.

It therefore rests with the teacher to know the way in which reading skill develops, the teaching sequences that are possible and the short-cuts that are permissible. To be able to pick and choose among teaching techniques and learning activities, the teacher must be very familiar with her subject. An experienced teacher is the best remedial teacher because she has an inner awareness of sequence in the programme around which she can vary the particular lessons.

The four main AIMS of a remedial programme are Acceleration, Intensive teaching, attention to Minutiae, and Sequence in an individualized programme. In addition there are three other guiding principles related to returning the child as an independent reader to his classroom. These complete a mnemonic: AIMS, ETC. The ETC refers to Extension, Transfer and Check-up.

Extension

The child who has failed to learn to read is also retarded in the creative writing and spelling of English, and possibly in the motor skill of writing. Activities in the remedial lessons should be planned so that these areas of written language also receive attention. This is not necessarily a matter of extending the period of remediation. It is a matter of good planning during the reading lessons so that writing activities are interwoven into the programme. They could become brakes on acceleration if used unwisely in the mistaken belief that repetitive copying will stamp in some image of the word. Words needed in sight vocabulary can, in part, be practised in spelling the most frequently used words in English.

The reading skill will always be ahead of the written language skills. In reading, the child should be meeting new words, trying new constructions, reading what he cannot hope to spell. However, if the child returns to his normal classroom as a proficient reader but is still unable to compete in written language activities his remediation has left him far from 'untangled'.

Transfer to Classroom Programme

Part of the intensive programme consists of close supervision by the teacher and this is not typical of the usual classroom because of numbers of children who need attention. There is, therefore, a weaning process as the remedial child is moved from dependence on the remedial teacher for checking his work, to partial independence where he checks what he can, to transfer back to the classroom where he has to be able to work entirely on his own, or to know when to appeal for assistance. Many children lose what they have gained in remedial lessons after transfer back to the classroom. It is one aim of the remedial programme to bring the child to a level of skill such that he can perform independently in the class he is returned to.

Check-up

Research studies which followed children who had remedial instruction have often reported that progress is not maintained in the classroom. It is essential that records be kept of the child's progress before and during remediation, of his status when transferred to the normal classroom and of re-tests at suitable intervals. It could be a characteristic of remedial programmes that as many as half the children transferred back should be picked up again for a 'refresher' course with the remedial teacher, a course much briefer than the first.

First Lessons in a Reading Recovery Programme

Do you know how reading is taught in your school? Do you know what reading processes are being trained in those children who succeed? You ought to. It is important information for anyone to have if they are to try to make judgements about the reading problems of the other pupils in the same school. Any reading programme has its 'risk areas', in that it stresses some facets of the reading process and must as a consequence give less attention to other aspects.

Early intervention calls for sensitive observation of the children making slow progress:

• In the context of the sequences of skill acquisition observed in the children making satisfactory progress.
• In the light of clear descriptions of the teaching, the day to day activities, and the sequential progressions of the programme.

I do not need an elaborate definition of reading difficulties. One simply takes the pupil — child, adolescent or adult — from where he is, to somewhere else. There is not one of us who could not read better if we had individual instruction in reading now.

Two assumptions are made in the outline that follows. The first is that a classroom programme will continue alongside the extra tuition. And the second is that the extra tutoring will be individual.

Step 1   A readable text

Find the hardest text the pupil can read with more than 90 percent accuracy. Don't guess. Measure it by taking a running record. This may mean that you use in descending order of difficulty

• an easy book
• a special interest book
• a story you have already read to this pupil
• a story that you write for this pupil using his known vocabulary
• a text which he dictated.

Each of these is moving one step closer to the child's limited horizons. The better he is the further up the sequence you can start. The poorer he is the lower down that sequence you should start. You cannot rely on a published sequence of material. That may be right on the average for children who succeed, but the teacher must be the expert chooser and sequencer of the texts for the reading recovery pupil. This is critical.

Step 2   Writing

Find out what he can write 'out of his head'. Keep his writing and reading programme moving forward in a reciprocal way (Clay, 1975).

Step 3   Record what he can do

Make notes on *what he can do*. Make yourself specify this. Put it into words. What does he do well? What strategies does he try? How does he help himself? What words, letters, sounds does he know?

Step 4   Build fluency on the very little he knows

Stay with what he knows; go over it in different ways until your ingenuity runs out, until he is moving fluently around this personal corpus of responses: the letters, words, messages read or written which he knows.

Hold his interest, bolster his confidence, make him your co-worker. Get the responding fluent and habituated. You will have founded your programme on a rock. Confidence, ease, habituation, flexibility and with luck discovery will be observed and even a straining at the leash so that he wants to go further. Don't move too soon; be sure the foundation is firm.

Step 5   New behaviours appear

Now you will probably notice some things emerging that you did not think the child knew. New and useful behaviours appear as he begins to relate things one to another. He remembers a book with this or that in it. A letter reminds him of his uncle's name. He reads *car* for *are* or some such mismatch that makes you feel he is getting closer to effective decisions about uncertainty.

There are two reasons for this appearance of new behaviours. The child has many strategies which he uses to solve problems in his daily life. He is now beginning to apply these to reading. Why didn't he do this before? When one is having difficulty with a task one tries several approaches. As each fails one ceases to try them. The failing reader has stopped using many strategies because he could not make them work. If you pitch the text at an easy level, and you support him in using the things he can do you will find that he begins to try again some of these discarded strategies. You should show delight at this spontaneous relating of 'this to that'.

So you unleash those discarded approaches this child has ceased to use on the text. You probably will not achieve this if you have pre-determined your programme or are using some author's published programme. But you will have more luck if you are responding to the child in an individual instruction situation. It only works well if the individual child's capacities determine the programme.

Step 6   Introduce new material

At this early stage there are some useful do's and don'ts which help to keep the task easy.

• Make sure the child can hear a distinction or difference between two sounds or two words before you teach him to *see* the difference.
• Start with large units not the smallest ones
— separate words out of phrases
— separate letters out of words.
• Encourage the use of hand and eye together. The use of the eyes alone comes later in the learning sequence.
• Link something the child does easily with something he finds hard (for support) before asking for the difficult response on its own.
• Teach by demonstration. Use a questioning approach only for established responses.
• Aim to teach a few *items* (letters, words, sounds) and then try to establish further examples by *strategies of comparison*. Teaching all the items in a category is a teacher's hang-up. What the child needs to know is a few items and some strategies for picking up new ones later, as he reads.

Step 7   Confusions

Now turn to the child's confusions. Without increasing the difficulty level and keeping to text reading, record and think about this particular child's confusions. Plan an attack on them. Talk to another couple of teachers about the easiest way to go from where he is to less confusion. That way you will find out what a blinkered approach each of us has to these difficulties and to teaching sequences. Probably you and your colleagues will not agree. Never mind. You have added their hypotheses to your own and can now approach the child's confusions tentatively, and with an open mind. With reading recovery cases do not rely on your own hunches. Be objective and critical of your own assumptions.

Some pointers about confusions are:

• Don't present them side by side. Get Item A well established and known for several weeks before you bring back Item B.
• Don't teach by the least noticeable difference principle. That is not the way we play 'Twenty Questions'.
• Is the child's difficulty in *seeing* a difference? If so, have him dictate, write, cut up and reassemble texts.
• Is the child's difficulty in *hearing* a difference? If so, articulate for him and with him very slowly, and teach him to use this strategy himself.
• Is the child's difficulty with order or sequence? If so, get him to dictate, read, cut up and reassemble and write a simple text.

You will probably have to move away from texts and into detail at this point. Resolve that this is a temporary but necessary detour, and plan to get back to text reading as soon as possible, preferably within the same lesson.

Step 8   A self-improving system

Plan to encourage a self-improving system and reinforce this.

• Give the child ways to detect error for himself.
• Encourage attempts to correct error.
• Give him clues to aid self-correction.
• Allow him to make checks or repetitions so he can confirm his first attempts.
• When he works out a word or text for himself, help him to know how he did it. Ask him 'How did you know?'.

See index.

Step 9   Increase text difficulty

Cautiously increase the text difficulty and repeat the sequence. Give massive practice on texts at this next level before you increase the difficulty level again.

Step 10   Now look at what he cannot do

Offer him many things. Start with what you think would have the greatest payoff. This might be:

• An intensive vocabulary spree.
• A training in predicting what structures come next.
• A training in hearing sound sequences, first and last sounds and clusters of sounds.
• A shift from sounding to syllabic attack.
• Letter identification.

Get those two colleagues together again and listen to their ideas on priorities and the way to achieve them. That exposes your assumptions to critical analysis. Keep the principles used in the games 'Twenty Questions' or 'Animal, Vegetable or Mineral', in mind.

Now go back to your pupil and ask him what he would like to learn next and try to work this in with your priorities.

Step 11 Some organizational points

Keep all those processes going *but* arrange for massive opportunity to read enchantingly interesting texts of just the right difficulty, over a longer period than anyone anticipated — and after the child and parents and class teacher want you to stop.

A typical tutoring session

A typical tutoring session would include each of these activities, usually in the following order. See page 70.

- re-reading of two or more familiar books — *text*
- letter identification
  (plastic letters on a magnetic board) — *letters*
- writing a story — *text*
- sound analysis of words
  (Elkonin technique) — *sounds*
- cut-up story to be rearranged — *text*
- new book introduced — *text*
- new book attempted — *text*

sound sequence

begin c̄ counters for isolated sounds

★ flexibility → arranging text in diff. sizes of space

When to Discontinue Tutoring

How can we decide whether a child is ready for discontinuing the individual tutoring? There can be no hard and fast criteria because the aim will be to replace a child in a class group in which he can continue to make progress, and this will differ from child to child and from school to school.

Consultation will be necessary — with the class teacher, the teacher in charge of the Junior School. Recorded observations of the child's behaviour during a class reading lesson will give important information for decisions about continuing or discontinuing tuition.

The Reading Recovery Project teachers found these questions helped them and those parents who had been associated with the recovery programme.

Setting

Is there an appropriate group at his level in his class?

Survival

Is this child ready to learn from group instruction? Will he continue to learn on his own in reading? Has he acquired some of the strategies in a self-improving system?

Running record analysis

Does he read increasingly difficult material always at 90 percent accuracy or above? Does he read (easy) books for pleasure?

Estimates of test score increases

Have you evidence which suggests that he will have improved on the tests of the Diagnostic Survey. Where was he weak before?

If discontinuing —

If you decide to discontinue tutoring prepare the child and his class teacher for this, perhaps working with the child in his classroom for the last two weeks of his programme.

Re-test the child on the Diagnostic Survey and analyse the strengths and weaknesses at this point in time. Compare them with the earlier testing and note the areas in which progress occurred. At this point decide to continue or to discontinue.

Discuss the child's current status with his class teacher.

Offer to monitor the child's progress, say once a fortnight or once a month, until you and his teacher are sure that he is continuing to make progress.

Expect to give a series of booster injections of instruction on an individual basis over the next two years.

A record sheet for recommending discontinuing is provided on page 113.

If not discontinuing —

The tutor-teacher may make a decision like one of the following:

• The child needs to continue in the full programme.
• The child needs further help in two or three areas where he is still weak; i.e. text reading, Elkonin analysis, word analysis, etc.
• The child needs further help to survive in the class situation.
• The child needs fewer and/or shorter lessons.
• The child needs one or two individual text reading sessions each week as a motivator, a check, to gain confidence, or any other reasons.

Set new learning goals. Aim to make the child independent. Continue only as long as necessary. Make new plans for discontinuing, testing only in the critical areas on this occasion.

Reading Recovery Teaching Procedures

These teaching procedures were developed with 6-year-old children who were unable to make satisfactory progress in their classrooms. It is unnecessary to teach most children in these ways.

The procedures are arranged so that a teacher can turn to the approach she requires for a particular child with a particular problem. Many of the suggestions that are detailed will not be appropriate for some children. As these procedures were being developed over a three year period we became convinced that the difficulties which children have in learning to read differ markedly from child to child; see Reading Recovery Research Project page 67. The teacher must skilfully select the activities needed by a particular child. Otherwise she will retard the child further by having him complete unnecessary work, thereby wasting precious learning time.

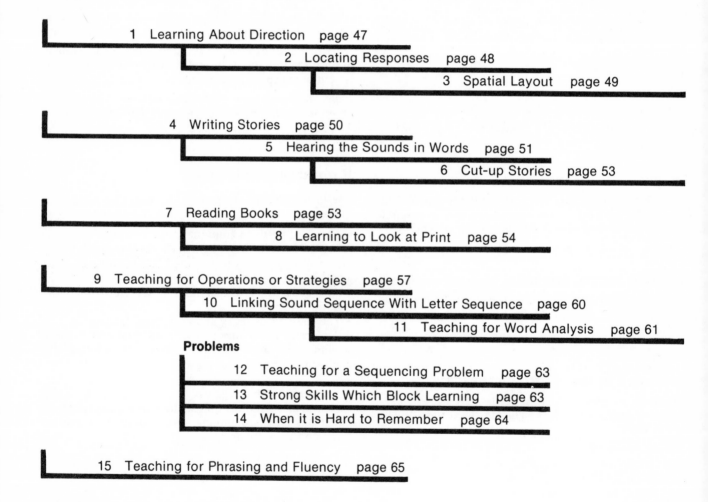

1:   Learning About Direction

Introduction

Directional confusions will be found in beginning readers who are learning the arbitrary rules we use to write down the English Language. They will also be found in some children having difficulty in learning to read. Two major contributing factors to persisting problems with direction are:

• That the child has learned and practised his peculiar directional habit for a long time.
• That the child has difficulty in learning movement patterns.

In our studies we have found that learning about direction can be very confusing for young children. The single recording procedures outlined here have helped our teachers to be sensitive observers of what children are learning about direction and print.

Record the child's directional responses to the print in a book with simple text. Ask the child to 'Read it with your finger'. Record any lapse from correct responding.

• Show the horizontal direction with arrows ⟶ ⟶
• Show the vertical direction by numbering the lines

   (3) ⟶
   (2) ⟶
   (1) ⟶

• Show whether the page was a left or right one Lp/Rp.
• Show whether the child used a left or right hand Lh/Rh.

A sample record might look like this

Page 1 ⟶ Lp
         ⟶ Lh

This would mean

Correct direction on a left page pointing with the left hand.

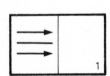

Page 2 ⟶ Rp
            Rh

On a right page with the right hand of the child moved from right-to-left and back on the next line from left-to-right.

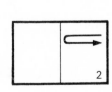

Page 3 ⟵ (2) Rp
        ⟵ (1) Rh

On a right page with the right hand the child moved from right to left and from bottom to top.

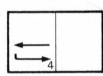

Page 4 ⟵ Lp
         ⟶ Lh

On a left page with the left hand the child moved from right to left and from left to right.

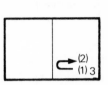

The (tentative) interpretation of this record might be:

• That the child had learned very little about the direction rules of print.
• That he used his left hand on a left page and his right hand on a right page.
• That a starting position at the top left of a page had not been established.
• That top to bottom direction was not consistent.

Recovery procedures

Starting position
Check each new book introduced to the child to see that the starting position on a page will not confuse this particular child.

• Accept either hand.
• Provide opportunities for overlearning and habituation.

Starting signal
Where the child moves incorrectly across print a signal such as a green sticker (Green light for Go) can be used to indicate the starting point to the left of the text.

◯ Tommy can ride

The child's working space may need this signal also. So be prepared to use it:

• On the blackboard.
• On the table top.
• On paper.

Some teachers are surprised when they find that a child who controls direction in one place uses different directional responses in another place.

To assist orientation on more complex text a coloured line or margin can be placed on the left side of the page.

> Tommy can ride
> on his tricycle
> down the road.

Choice of texts

The child should learn to do without these signals as soon as he has gained stable control over starting position. He will be helped at this point by the use of texts in which the layout is similar.

As the child gains control over direction more variable layout should then be introduced to ensure that he becomes flexible in his approach to print. Aim for stable control over direction before you push for flexibility.

Goal

The goal is a particular movement pattern suited to books, blackboards, paper and all print. It has probably been achieved when the child

- uses either hand to point to print
- on either page
- without lapse in direction
- or with self-correction following a lapse.

Talking about direction

As an intermediate step it may be necessary for the child to guide his own movement with words that remind him of what to do. This must be unlearned later because the movement pattern must become a habit that is used automatically without requiring the child to attend to it.

So, avoid talking about these action patterns if possible. Model the action for the child as often as he needs this help.

2:   Locating Responses

Introduction

Young children have difficulty pointing to a row of objects in sequence one after the other. This has been accepted as important in early mathematics lessons but few have noted that this is also a limitation for reading. It may mean that the child cannot attend to one printed word at a time in sequential order.

Most school entrants can do this or will quickly learn to do this in the first year at school. A few children having difficulty with learning to read will need special help in learning these responses.

Ask a child to point to each word in a simple one line text. If he fails to do this there may be several reasons. Only one reason is considered here; he cannot *attend to, focus on* or *point to* one word after the other.

Use some exercises like those that follow to establish these behaviours.

Recovery procedures

Early learning

One after the other put down two objects in a row. Call the child's attention to them and point to them one after the other, the left one first. *Don't count them.*

Ask the child to *point* to a row of three objects; four objects; five objects or more; in sequence one after the other. Record:

- The starting point.
- The direction.
- Any difficulties.

Intermediate steps

Repeat the exercise with objects and sequences like felt dots, geometric shapes, pencil dots, two letter words (same and different), five word sentences. *It is probably wise to avoid using single letters.* Record:

- The starting point.
- The direction.
- Any difficulties.

Provide practice, using the appropriate directional pattern for print.

The goal is coordinated, one-to-one correspondence with the movement pattern needed for print and pointing to individual symbols in a set.

Now ask the child to tell you about the objects in sequence. Without pointing:

- Name the objects.
- Name the colour of the dots.
- Give the number of dots.

Advanced learning

Words and spaces on books with:

- One line per page.
- Two lines per page.
- More than two lines.

If the child needs help to *see* the words and spaces between words write out a line or two of the text of the book in large print exaggerating the spaces.

Cut the sentence up into single words as the child watches. Get the child to remake the sentence and reread it several times, pointing carefully.

You can rearrange the cut-out words with *over-emphasized spaces at first,* gradually reducing these to normal spacing.

To develop an accurate locating response on book texts for the child who still has difficulties:

- Use two-finger framing (with two index fingers).
- Use a long pointer. (It requires more effort to control the movement.)
- Encourage deliberate voice pointing.

The extra control needed to accomplish these more difficult motor tasks slows down speech so that the child feels the pauses between the spoken words while his fingers show the boundaries of the written words.

Work for flexibility
Once a good locating response has been established on a familiar book with two-finger framing get the child to read with one-finger pointing.

If you are using cut-up stories — the child's stories that are written out and cut up — these can be rearranged by the teacher in several ways — one line, two lines, three lines, to foster this flexibility:

- I went to the zoo.
- I went
  to the zoo.
- I went
  to the
  zoo.

Take the opportunity to ask the child to read a few words of the story on each rearrangement.

As a more advanced task cut-up stories can be rearranged *by the child*. The teacher alters the size of the space in which the child is asked to remake the story.

- making it larger   I   am   a   big   girl
- making it progressively smaller   I am a
                                     big girl

The children who have most difficulty with learning about direction tend to have problems with this type of task.

Too many breaks
Over-segmenting can cause difficulties with one to one correspondence. For example

A	way	we	go
Away	we	go	to

To overcome a bad case of too many breaks exaggerate the segments with magnetic letters spatially and also with shouting or singing, then gradually rejoin the two segments again.

A — way
Away

Caution. For most children the activities described in this section will be unnecessary. They learn these things incidentally while exploring books in a more enjoyable way.

There is no point in delaying a child's progress with such a detailed programme unless these activities have value for a particular problem that has not responded to other approaches.

3:   Spatial Layout

Introduction

In trying to write stories some children have become very confused about how to use the space on the page. Perhaps this stems from their confused concepts of the relationships of letters to words. If the child shows confusion these activities may help.

Recovery procedures

With letters and words
- In word study use *magnetic letters* to overlearn the positioning of letters in making a word. Exaggerate the space between letters in some well known words and get the child to return them to the normal spacing.
- Use *magnetic letters* to accentuate the spaces between words and get the child to return them to normal spacing.

In writing
- *In writing* help the child to leave a finger space between words, saying 'It is easier for us to read'.
- Give the child help to use the space on the page in spacing his sentences. This help might mean giving a definite starting position — top left hand corner.

In cut-up stories
- *In cut-up stories* help the child to remake the story several times, each time altering the space in which he is working so that he is forced to recognize the layout of the story to fit the 'spatial frame' which you have created by your use of the table top.

The aim in these activities is to give the child the ability to organize himself in relation to written language space. Therefore any aids and props should be used only for the period for which they are essential.

An important note
We have not found lined paper a help. It seems to impose too many constraints on the child who has difficulty with spatial learning or with confusions. But cues and prompts as aids on the blank unlined paper work well.

4:   Writing stories

Introduction

Many of the operations needed in early reading are practised in another form in early writing.

This is not a matter of copying words and stories: it concerns going from ideas to spoken words to printed messages.

First lessons in a reading recovery programme will have explored what letters and words the child can write. From a very few these should be expanded as quickly as letter learning will allow.

Elkonin analysis and word building with magnetic letters are also supportive activities for early writing.

These should be concurrent activities. They need not precede the introduction of child-dictated stories (see Clay, 1975).

The focus of these procedures is on getting the child to produce his own written stories.

Recovery procedures

For these stories reading recovery teachers used unlined exercise books, turned sideways. The child drew the picture and wrote his story on the page nearest him. His attempts to write words, teacher-written models or Elkonin boxes were all placed in the top page.

| Working space for teaching and trials |
| Child's story |

Child dictates a story

The child is invited to tell a story (sentence) about the previous book read or about the best part of the story, or about some topic of interest to him.

Talk with the child about

- something he has done
- a story he has heard or read
- a TV programme he has seen
- something that interests him
- an experience you have had together.

Suggest that he draws a picture about it. Provide felt pens, coloured pencils, ballpoint pens for him to choose from. (This activity will gradually take up less time as writing confidence grows. Eventually the picture can be omitted.)

Encourage him to tell you a story (sentence) about it. Repeat the child's story. Scribble down the sentence for your own reference.

Sometimes you may want to help the child to word the sentence so that it contains words he can write, but do this very rarely.

Child writes

Encourage the child to write as much as he can alone each session. Praise him for his efforts. The child writes the words he knows using his practice page. Write some of the easier words on the practice page for him to copy. Write the difficult words into the story for him.

Get fluency

When the child writes a word you want him to know next time say, *'Do it again. And again. Now write it here. And here. Do it faster. Once more.'*

This procedure helps the child to practise producing the *sequence* of letters needed for that word.

- It builds fluency.
- It helps the child to remember the word in every detail.

Come back to this word again next day, or for several days asking each time for the same fluent writing.

Later

- When he comes to a problem word help him to attend to and isolate at least the initial sound and to predict what he would expect to see at the beginning. Then write the word for him to copy.
- Use Elkonin analysis techniques (see page 51).

Errors in stories

One way to approach this problem is:

- allow the child to finish
- show him how you would write it on the blackboard
- get him to watch and say the word slowly as you slide a masking card along the word, exposing a letter or letter cluster at a time
- emphasize the matching of sounds and letters.

Note: Accept the child's phonemic analysis (sound analysis) as evidence of the stage he is at.

Re-reading

Get the child to re-read the story pointing word by word. Or re-read his story with him.

Type out the story

Whatever the child writes can be typed out for him to read before too long an interval. A bulletin typewriter (large type) is useful for young readers. The larger type of some electric 'golf-balls',* used with generous spacing is an alternative.

*   IBM Typehead Gothic Code 005 10 pitch spacing

Resist the urge to edit this story or to elaborate it. Change as little of the child's story as is consistent with good teaching. Paste this typed version into the child's unlined exercise book for revision reading.

5: Hearing the Sounds in Words

Introduction

The aim of these activities is to help the child think about the order of sounds in spoken words. In Elkonin's view (1973) the sound is the reality and how the word is written is a model for the reality. In spelling a language we use different sets of letter clusters to write the same sound. A beginning reading programme brings most children to an awareness of sound sequences in words rather effortlessly.

We have worked with some children who find it extraordinarily difficult to hear the sounds that go to make up words. For example, some children consistently focus on the final sound of a word, and for them, this completely masks the initial sounds.

The teacher has to work with such children individually and act as an analyser of words into sounds. This is analogous to acting as his scribe at first when he cannot write. The teacher articulates the words very slowly and gradually develops the same skill in her pupil.

It is an essential feature of the theory behind this tutoring to hear the sounds in words and that the child's first lessons take place *in the absence of letters and/or printed words*. He must hear the word spoken and try to break it into its sounds. He is asked to indicate what he hears by using *counters* not *letters*.

If a child needs help in hearing the sounds in words he should begin at the beginning of these recovery procedures and work slowly or rapidly through the early stages according to his needs.

Recovery procedures

It is useful to have prepared cards for words of two, three and four *sounds* (not letters) and to have a selection of counters and buttons.

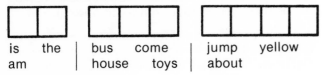

| is   the | bus   come | jump   yellow |
| am | house toys | about |

Early learning
Hearing syllables
Ask the child to clap the syllables in words distinguishing one and two-syllable words and sometimes three. Repeat

this as opportunities arise in stories and in word study.

Hearing the sounds
A teacher would expect a child who is having difficulty to attempt only two or three of the following activities in the first lessons.

- Slowly and deliberately articulate the word for the child. Let the child hear those sounds that can be separated in a natural way.
- Ask the child to articulate it for himself aloud. Ask him to 'say it slowly'. This transfers the initiative for the activity to him.
- Ask the child to watch your lips while you say it, and then copy you.
- Use the prepared cards with squares on them and push counters into those 'boxes' as you articulate the segments of the word slowly for the child.

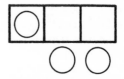

The illustration would serve for any word of three sounds (r-u-n). Be careful. Think about this in setting up the task. You need *a square for every sound* and NOT for every letter. At this stage, it is an aural task. It has nothing to do with spelling.

Now try to get the child to do this. Articulate the word slowly for him while he move the counters. Repeat the task several times.

As long as the child finds the coordination of *saying slowly* and *pushing counters* too difficult, it may be necessary for the teacher to share the articulation and the counter pushing, changing roles to enable the child to practise both parts.

To introduce this activity it is helpful to have a few picture cards for simple words such as   *cat   bus   hen   pig*   with accompanying boxes. But before long the child will be working on a much larger vocabulary.

Intermediate steps
Hearing sounds and writing letters
When a child can push counters into the boxes as he says the sounds and when he has a good grasp of letter identification, he is ready to make another kind of model of the sound segments in words, using letters.

On the blackboard or in his unlined exercise book the teacher draws a box for each *sound* in the word to be analysed. It may be a word he wants to write or a new word for a book that is being introduced.

Words with more than four sounds present difficulties and might be avoided as analysis exercises until the child gains skill in hearing sounds.

● Articulate the word for him slowly, emphasizing the sounds. For the child with little control,ask him to watch your lips.

● Help the child to articulate the sound segments of the word in this manner. Use a mirror if you want to make the child aware of what his lips and tongue are doing.

● Draw a box for each sound segment.

● Encourage the child to articulate the sounds and point to the boxes you have drawn, accepting a gross approximation at first.

● Ask 'What letters would you expect to see?' Write in the letters for him.

● *Accept any correct sound despite its location* and write it in the correct position as the child watches. Then use questions to locate other letters.

● Accept the sounds in any order.

● He will not necessarily begin to identify them from first to last.

● Prompt with questions like:

What do you hear at the beginning?
What do you hear at the end?
What else can you hear?
What do you hear in the middle?

The teacher can act as scribe to produce words like these.

B	i	ll

b	oa	t

The child may write only those letters he knows.

Alternatively, the teacher may get the child to fill in what he can himself and then complete the word for him, perhaps *teaching one new point* but not explaining everything.

t	r		ck

truck

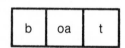

m			s	t	

monster

Note on consonants and vowels

Be satisfied if he can separate out some of the consonants. Give the child the vowels as these seem to be much more difficult to hear and require more experience with reading and writing.

For the teacher who is not used to a linguist's analysis of the sounds of spoken English *there are traps* in this activity. For example, one child responding well to her own phonemic analysis of *cousins*, wrote:

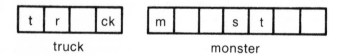

Kusns

Except for the *Ss* which should have been *Zs* this is an accurate rendering of the sounds in the word but not one which helped the child to reach the written form of the word. It was an inappropriate word for training sound to letter analysis.

The teacher must be alert to detect the difference between what is good analysis of sounds and what is confusion or error. Here are some examples of accurate 'hearing' by children which should not be undervalued.

plac	aftr	childrn
(place)	(after)	(children)

Advanced learning
Hearing sounds in words — further transitions
After the early learning and intermediate steps the child is ready for an important transition.

I At this stage we introduce the child to the mismatch between the sounds of the language to which he has been attending and the way we spell the words. Now we want to provide the child with a box for each letter, even though two letters may not represent two sounds.

One of our teachers found an easy way to introduce the transition. She drew enough boxes for the sounds only but she put in a dotted line to divide any box that needed two letters like this

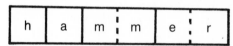

h	a	m	m	e	r

and then gradually transferred to solid lines.

Explain the shift to the child — a box for every letter he needs.

● Articulate the word clearly for the child. Let him hear the segments in sequence several times.

● Make a squared diagram in his booklet with spaces equal to the number of *letters* required.

● Help the child to fill in the letters of the word using stress or pausing on a sound in an exaggerated way to emphasize the sound you want him to focus on.

● As soon as the child can attend to the sound, return to a natural rate and mode of articulation.

● Find similar sound segments in known words.

moth<u>er</u>
monst<u>er</u>

● Help the child if the word has unusual elements or those that he is not yet ready for (especially vowels).

II Make another special transition as soon as possible. Have the child fill in the letters *in sequence*. This requires him to use new ways of analysing the word he is trying to write.

III As the child becomes a better reader he will still continue to encounter new words and the following activities would still be needed from time to time.

- The child hears the teacher slowly articulating the sounds in sequence, perhaps several times.
- The teacher may ask the child to watch her lips and say it with her.
- The teacher may use a mirror to show the child how she makes the sounds.
- Encourage the child to 'say it slowly'.
- Use stress to emphasize a sound you want him to focus on.
- Use pausing on that sound or draw it out in an exaggerated way to call attention to it.

The writing of the word in boxes will not be needed very often at this stage.

6: Cut-up Stories

Introduction

The first cut-up stories may be written by the teacher from the child's dictation but usually a teacher asks the child to re-read his story from his unlined book so that she can write it again on paper.

Cut up the story into language units which you know the child will be able to reassemble. Use larger segments for poorer readers. The descending order of size will be phrases, words, structural segments, or clusters of letters, and single letters.

If you want to cut up a word into syllables ask the child to clap the syllables of the word to show you where to cut up the word.

Get the child to reassemble the cut-up story. This usually calls for careful self-monitoring and checking but it can be made easy or difficult. Assembly

- on top of the model is a matching response — EASY.
- below the model is a matching response — HARDER.
- without the model is a reading response — HARD.

Get the child to scan for errors. If he made errors, say 'Something's not quite right' calling for a self-monitoring response.

Get the child to re-read with careful word by word matching to the syllable level if this was used.

An example
- The child was invited to pick out the best part of the story.
- The teacher offered to write that story for him. She wrote it twice.
(An important link between text in books and writing activities is emphasized by this simple act.)
- The child pointed to 'A' and said he could do that one.
(The teacher had missed an opportunity to have him

write what little he knew.)
- The teacher read the written text and modelled pointing behaviour.
- The child tried inaccurately.
- The teacher guided his hand.
- The child tried accurately.
- The teacher cut up one copy of the story, starting with the first word, emphasizing its word components by reading each word as she chopped it off.
- The child reassembled the story matching it on top of the second story. It became a *visual matching* exercise rather than a *reading task*. The last word *bus* was matched but re-oriented 180°.
- The teacher asked him to turn it around and put the tall one on that (left) side. Note that he knew *s* and in *snq* it is correctly oriented.

Cut-up stories provide the child with practice for

- assembling sentences
- one-to-one correspondence (of words spoken and written)
- directional behaviours
- checking behaviours
- breaking oral language into segments
- word study (from cut-up words)

and it is a puzzle-type task on known text that can be used for home practice. The written story in the blank page exercise book provides the correct model.

7: Reading Books

Introduction

The critical difficulty for some children who seem to have many particular skills and a fair grasp of certain items of knowledge is the using of such assets in the sequential sorting process of reading continuous text. The reading recovery procedures provide three opportunities for fostering integration of skills — in reading text (see below), in writing and re-reading his own stories (see page 50), in reconstructing cut-up versions of those stories (see above).

Recovery procedures

Choice of book
Choose the reading book very carefully. Keep to a text that is well within the child's item knowledge, that is using words he can read and letters he can identify when he needs to use them as cues. There should be a minimum of new things to learn if the teaching goal is the integration of all these skills.

Orientation to the story before reading

Introduce the book and make the child familiar with the *plot, the words, the sentences and the writing style.* For example, a teacher might:

- Draw the child's attention to the important ideas.
- Discuss the pictures of the *whole* book.
- Give opportunities for the child to *hear* the new words which he will have to guess from the pictures and language context.
- Ask him to find one to two new and important words in the text after he has said what letter he would expect to see at the beginning.

This effort to facilitate responding, might be explained in terms like recency and familiarity. Another explanation is that the teacher is ensuring that the child has in his head, the ideas and the language he needs to produce when prompted in sequence by print cues.

Reading the book with help

Prepared by this the child reads the new material as independently as is possible. (Perhaps only half the book would be read on the first occasion.) The overall aim is to provide opportunities for independent attack and for teacher confirmation and reinforcement of appropriate behaviours.

Encourage strong, definite locating behaviours getting the child to point to each word with the index finger to achieve crisp word-by-word integration of point-say-look behaviours.

Support the child with any particular features that are likely to cause him difficulty. For example, provide a model which emphasizes by stress, shouting, singing or some other means the anticipated difficulty. In this example *early* was expected to present a particular child with a problem.

> The daisy is asleep
> EARLY in the morning.

Or with minimum help

With a child who is using cues appropriately from all areas, and is on the way to independence say, '*I want you to look at all the pictures and tell me what the story is about. Then I want you to read it all by yourself. I am not going to help unless you really can't do it.*'

Accompany the child's pointing with your own pointer and fail to move on when he makes an error that you see he could self-correct. Sound the initial letter if necessary.

Comment positively when the child corrects himself. Reinforce self-correction especially if the child tries to use the kind of cue he has previously avoided. Talk about self-correction. Say how you like it.

Second reading for fluency

Re-read the story with the child, for a second time in the same *lesson* to get fluency and a flow of words. Hopefully time will allow for this. As you read stay one step behind the child on problem words to check his mastery of them.

Home and school practice

Accumulate a box of familiar books and re-read a selection of these each session, say two at the beginning of the lesson. The practice encourages confidence and fluency in bringing reading behaviours together. Get the child to read books at home for independent practice.

A child who is on the way to independence needs as many books as possible at his level. Allow the child to learn to read by reading many books.

Re-reading of book

When a book has been introduced, read, and practised at home, be ready to check it for accuracy at the next session. Check out any remaining errors with word analysis exercises such as:

- Use of structural features, s, ed, ing.
- Matching with finger.
- Segmenting the sentence or word.
- Asking 'What letters do you expect to see?'

Here is an example of a check on a known book.

- The teacher reads the title, *Who are you?* and asks the child to read it with his finger. The teacher can observe directional behaviour and speech-to-print matching. The child is invited to organize and control his own reading behaviour independently.
- The child reads the book and the teacher takes a Running Record.
- The child reads *bears* for *elephants* and corrects himself. The teacher says, '*What does elephants start with?*' an invitation for aural analysis of *e* in *elephants* and a sound-to-letter association.
- The teacher quickly checks some knowledge of individual words which were teaching points for this book. She uses a sliding mask card to efficiently and swiftly isolate the word, and asks '*What is that?*' The child responds with speed. She includes a question about punctuation, *a question mark.*
- This book is placed in the child's box of books he has read.

8: Learning to Look at Print

Introduction

A child who only knows a few letters and words is probably not using visual signposts or cues. Ways of looking at print and searching for cues must be established. Most children will discover all that they need to know as they read books. A few children take a very passive approach to print. They need more help in learning about print.

Recovery procedures

Looking at print — early learning
Start from the known and move out very slowly to anything new.
The known will be:

- The child's name.
- A few words which he can read and/or write.
- One or two particular books.
- The child's dictated story.

From the focus of the child's vocabulary the teaching can slowly move towards extending the child on each activity above.

Here is a first lesson in a recovery programme built around the child's name. The teacher uses three ways of directing the child's attention to visual features of print.

The teacher says *'Make your name here,'* but the child makes no response. The teacher begins to write the child's name.

She pays attention to the first letter, saying, *'We make it like this.'*

She models the movements vertically in the air.

Three ways of remembering

1 Movement	The teacher holds the child's hand and guides him. This identifies the letters by *movement*.
2 Words	*'Down and around'* she says. This is a *verbal* description of movement.
3 Visual Form	She writes the letter in his book. She may ask the child to write it. This is a *visual* model.

The teacher writes the rest of the child's name and he copies this. From this the child learns some specific letters:

- How to put them in a set sequence.
- Several features of letters, usable in other letters.
- Several features of words.

Suggestions for extending his knowledge of words
- Have the child make a word out of magnetic letters. Jumble it and remake it until the child can do this fluently.
- Write the word in big print for him.
- Ask the child to trace the word with finger contact saying each part of the word as he traces it.
- Use a paint-brush and water to make a disappearing word on the blackboard.
- Use a wet crayon to make a magic 'appearing' word on the blackboard.

The next suggestion is a very important one.

- Ask the child to write the word many times getting fluency and overlearning.
- Keep these words in mind to use in other activities.

Gradually extend the child's writing vocabulary. A useful initial vocabulary can be selected from

Child's name, I, a, is, in, am, to, come, like, see.

These words help with the stories the child tries to write and with the first books he can read. Try to keep all words within the vocabulary that he controls, and slowly add to this.

Reading recovery teachers have found it useful to build up vocabulary charts for individual children to be read, referred to, and added to during lessons.

Another idea is to build up a box of word cards indexed by letters of the alphabet.

Suggestions for extending his knowledge of letters
At first use only the letters the child can already identify. Give him lots of practice with these.
- Allow the child to label letters in *any* appropriate way — by name, by sound, or by word beginning. We find good readers use all three ways of identifying letters. It seems to be useful to have more than one way of labelling a letter, and we suggest that you do not insist on only one type of label being used.
- Have the child run over the new letter with his finger to feel the shape. Identify the letter by name. Talk about the similarity/dissimilarity of the capital and lower case forms.
- Model the formation of the new letter with chalk on the blackboard writing in large print and directing the movements verbally.
- Giving him verbal instructions, and guiding his hand if necessary, have the child write the letter

-in the air
-on the blackboard
-on paper.

Teachers in our programme developed many interesting activities for drawing children's attention to the features of letters such as sticky coloured paper cut-outs, formation cards showing where to start letters, tracing paper activities, and so on.

Work for flexibility:

- Use vertical and horizontal surfaces.
- Use different mediums — felt pen, chalk, magnetic letters.
- For a particular child use unusual mediums — sandpaper or felt letters.
- Use different sizes of print.
- Look for a simple book that illustrates the new letter (such as a Price-Milburn skill builder) and read through it, emphasizing the initial sounds.
- Get the child to identify the letter by an object which he identifies with the new letter. (It might be a picture from the book.)
- Go through his alphabet book (see the end of this section) to show him where the new letter fits in sequence and draw the key picture and the letter forms.
- Teach a new word starting with that letter.

Every new thing learned should be revised in several other activities.

When children confuse letters

Some children have well-established habits of confusing letters. One way to help them control and monitor these unwanted responses on the one hand, and develop the desirable new responses on the other, is to bring the behaviour under verbal direction for a short time. This practice must be used sensitively. It is a temporary device which, if continued too long will itself become an unwanted response, slowing up the automatic responding required.

- Attend to similarities and differences of letters.
- Use three-dimensional forms such as magnetic letters and create clear demonstrations of any distinctions that the child should learn.
- Put three of four examples of the same letter onto the magnetic board. Jumble the forms with some known letters and have the child find 'all the *E*'s' and put them in a line.

Because it takes reading recovery children some time to distinguish letters revise new learning frequently. As they become very familiar with some letters those letters can be omitted from the practice exercises.

There are many ways in which letters can be paired, and grouped. Games can be invented to suit particular children, but don't waste time on unnecessary games.

Attend to the forming of letters which are confused

Draw the child a model on the blackboard slowly, directing the movements verbally. Ask the child to try, and guide his hand if necessary. Verbalize the movement (e.g. *'Make k down, and in and out'*). Try to bring the child's movements under your verbal control and then transfer this verbal control to the child. Continue to practise after the child gives the correct response and revise often.

Attend to common faults

The child sometimes adopts an awkward starting position, for example. If this is important direct attention to it. Be firm about essentials, that is, whatever your most important teaching points are, ignore other inadequacies. You cannot afford to overteach on non-essentials. It costs too much in motivation.

Letter names

You may direct the child's attention to movement or to visual shape. But if you want to talk about the letters it usually helps to use letter names. They seem to act as a shorthand type of label representing many other experiences with letters.

Three important points

Letter learning for most children is done incidentally as they learn to read stories. Special help with letter learning for reading recovery children must not become an end in itself. It is a minor part of a recovery programme. The child cannot afford to waste time on letter games when he could be reading well-chosen books. Careful judgement is needed to give the child just enough opportunity to gain control of letter identification.

In many cases of letter confusion an appropriate strategy is to help the child gain control of *one* of the confusing letters before introducing the second. It does not help most children to work on confusing letters side by side.

The aim is to have a child recognize letters as rapidly as we do without any props. He needs to end up with a fast recognition response. Be careful that your teaching leads to this.

An alphabet book

Early learning

It is usually desirable to take stock of and tidy up a child's knowledge of the alphabet. One idea that works well with children having difficulty is to make a paper book which will allow the alphabet to be printed in sequence, with a drawing for each letter the child knows. Use the form of the letter that the child already knows, capital or lower case.

When a child knows 20 or more letter symbols write *these letters only* in the alphabet book leaving gaps for letters yet to be learned. Use a key picture which the child himself identifies with that letter already.

The child has a feel for the size of the task, how far he has gone, what he knows for certain and as the letters not yet known are flipped over, he must feel that it is important to be sure of and use what he knows and to overlook for the present, some of the difficulties.

The child's own alphabet book has proved more useful than published books we have tried. Yet for the child having little difficulty with reading, a beautifully illustrated alphabet book would be an enriching experience.

Advanced learning
When the child has fairly extensive control over letter knowledge practise sequencing the alphabet by getting him to give the consecutive letter before you turn to that page.

Teacher (pointing):	a — apple
Child (anticipating):	b — balloon
	(Turn the page)

Teacher (pointing):	c — cat
Child (anticipating):	d — dog
	(Turn the page)

Avoid saying *'a is for apple'* because many children try to find a printed sign for *is for*.

9: Teaching for Operations or Strategies

Good readers
Reading instruction often focusses on items of knowledge — words, letters, sounds. Most children respond to this teaching in active ways. They search for links between the items and they relate new discoveries to old knowledge. They operate on print as Piaget's children operate on problems, searching for relationshps which order the complexity of print and therefore simplify it. For such children the teaching sequence described below is unnecessary.

Poor readers
Children who fail to progress in reading do not approach print in this way. The operations which they have tried to carry out have not brought order to the complexity and they have often become passive in their confusion.

This section offers suggestions which have proved useful in getting passive poor readers to become more active in searching for cues, predicting possible responses and verifying these responses.

A self-improving system
The end-point of such instruction is reached when children have a self-improving system — a set of operations just adequate for reading a slightly more difficult text for the precise words and meanings of the author.

When we operate or work on a problem we are engaged in a conscious search for solutions. In reading we sometimes consciously search for a word or a meaning or a correction but most of the time our active search is a fast reaction of the brain that seems to be automatic and not conscious. Perhaps strategies is a better name for these fast actions used in reading.

Recovery procedures: operations or strategies used on texts

A child can only acquire and practise these important operations or strategies on texts as he reads books and re-reads the stories he has written. The earliest strategies are simple. They are important because they give the child a means of checking that he is attending to the right part of the page. They are:

1 Directional movement
Ideas for encouraging appropriate directional behaviours have been described already under Learning About Direction (page 47).

2 One to one matching
This was discussed in detail under Locating Responses (page 48). Here are some ways to encourage this as the child reads books.

- Say *'Read it with your finger.'*
  Or *'Did that match?'*
  Or *'Were there enough words?'*
  Or *'Did you run out?'*
- Accompany the child's pointing with your own pointer and fail to move on when he makes an error that you feel he could self-correct.
- When you want to slow down a too-fluent language response, use two small pieces of card or two fingers to frame each word.

3 Locate one or two known words
Encourage the child to locate items he knows in the text:

- Read back an error sentence and ask *'Is that right?'*
- Re-read the previous word or words with fluent phrasing and stop at the problem word.
- Re-read the previous phrase leading up to the problem word fluently, and articulate the first sound of the problem word.

4   Locate an unknown word
   As in (3) above.

Checking on oneself or self-monitoring

• To encourage self-monitoring in the very early stages ask the child to go back to one to one pointing:
Say *'Point to each one.'*
Or   *'Use a pointer and make them match.'*
• Direct the child's attention to meaning:
Say *'Look at the picture.'*
Or   *'What happened in the story when...'*
• For particular attention to an error allow the child to continue to the end of the sentence:
Say   *'I liked the way you did that.*
         But can you find the hard bit?'
Or   *'I liked the way you did that.*
       You found the hard bit.
       Where was it?'
• If the child gives signs of uncertainty — hesitation, frowning, a little shake of the head — even though he takes no action:
Say *'Was that OK?'*
Or   *'Why did you stop?'*
Or   *'What did you notice?'*

   These questions tell the child that you want him to monitor his own reading. The operation to be learned is checking on oneself.

•   Don't forget to reinforce the child for his self-monitoring attempts whether they are successful or not:
Say *'I liked the way you tried to work that out.'*
• Cues from letter sequences.
Let the child predict the word he expects it to be. Cover the problem word and ask:
   'What do you expect to see:
       at the beginning?
       at the end?
       in the middle?
       after the m?'
Ask him to check as you uncover the word.
• Ask the child *'Were you right?'*
after both correct and incorrect words.
Ask *'How did you know?'* after correct words.

• Encourage the child to *'Try that again'* indicating where to begin a re-run and implying that he search for cues you think he will find.

Cross-checking
When the child can monitor his own reading and can search for and use structure or message or sound cues begin to encourage him to check one kind of cue against another.
• Point up discrepancies between two sources of cues.

Say *'It could be ... but look at ...'*
Or insert possible words until the child can confirm the response using initial and final letters.
Or say *'Check to see if what you read looks right and sounds right to you.'*

An example of fostering checking behaviour
T   *'What was the new word you read?'*
Ch   *'Bicycle'*
T   *'How did you know it was bicycle?'*
Ch   *'It was a bike'* (semantics)
T   *'What did you expect to see?'*
Ch   *'A "b"?'*
T   *'What else?'*
Ch   *'A little word, but it wasn't'*
T   *'So, what did you do?'*
Ch   *'I thought of bicycle'*
T   (Reinforcing the checking)
'Good, I liked the way you worked at that all by yourself.'

Outcome — The child will attend to checking because the teacher attended to it.

Searching for cues
To develop a search for more specific types of cues reading recovery teachers used these questions.

• Cues in sentence structure (syntax):
   Say *'You said... Does that sound right?'*
   Or *'Can you say it that way?'*
• Cues from the message (semantics):
   Say *'You said... Does that make sense?'*
• Cues from the letters (graphic cues):
   Say *'Does it look right?'*
• Or more generally:
   Say *'What's wrong?'*

   If the child has a bias towards letter detail the teacher's prompts will be directed towards the message and the language structure.

• She may need to orient the child to the picture as a meaning source.
• She may need to induce the word as when the problem word was broth and the teacher said, *'There was an old lady who lived in a shoe...'* and the child said, *'I know — soup!'*
• Sometimes it is necessary for a child to gain control over a particular language structure first, so that he can bring it back to the reading situation.

Four types of cue
From the theory of reading behind these recovery procedures there are four types of cue any two of which may be cross-checked to confirm a response. They can be represented by a square.

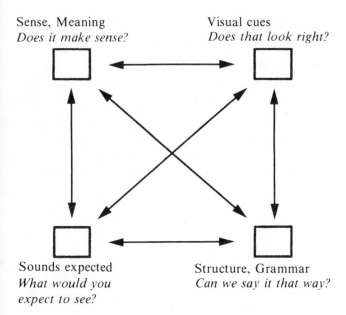

Sense, Meaning
Does it make sense?

Visual cues
Does that look right?

Sounds expected
What would you expect to see?

Structure, Grammar
Can we say it that way?

An example of fostering searching behaviour

T *'You almost got that page right. There was something wrong with this line. See if you can find what was wrong.'*
Ch (Child silently re-reads checking)
'I said Lizard but it's Lizard's'.
T *'How did you know?'*
Ch *'Cause it's got an "s".'*
T *'Is there any other way we could know?'* (Search further)
Ch (Child re-runs in whisper)
*'It's funny to say 'Lizard dinner'!
It has to be Lizard's dinner like Peter's dinner, doesn't it?'*
T (Reinforcing the searching) *'Yes. That was good. You found two ways to check on that tricky new word.'*

Outcome — The child will attend to searching because the teacher attended to it.

Self-correction

The child who monitors his own reading searches for cues and cross-checks at least two types of information, will be self-correcting some of his own errors.

• Comment positively on self-correction
   Say *'I liked the way you found out what was wrong all by yourself.'*
• Allow time for self-correction. The child must take the initiative.
• To make a child even more independent of the teacher don't do anything when he makes a mistake or stops.

Don't give him any clues.
   Say *'You made a mistake on that page. Can you find it?'*
This places the responsibility on the child.

A note on verbalizing the process

Check on some words accurately read with *'How did you know?'* or *'Were you right?'*

   In familiar tasks a young child often comes to a stage where he can comment on what he can do. The question *'How did you know it was X?'* invites the child to examine his own behaviour, after he has successfully carried out some operation in his reading. The teacher may know what cues he used and may want him to verbalize this. Or she may be asking for the child's help so that she can understand this particular strength he has.

   What is the relationship between the need for fast, automatic responses to words and phrases, and this instructional device which slows up the process and asks the child to think about it? It seems legitimate to encourage a child to verbalize a strategy or a principle or a rule-like consistency because these have more general application. They have generative value. It also seems legitimate to bring to a child's notice a success he has had in mastering a previous difficulty, because confidence has generative value only.

   It is a tactic that could be overworked and could interfere with the automatic responding that goes with fluency.

The goal is a self-improving system

Teachers aim to produce independent readers whose reading improves whenever they read. In independent readers

• early strategies are secure and habituated
• the child *monitors* his own reading
• he *searches* for cues in word sequences, in meaning, in letter sequences
• he *discovers* new things for himself
• he *cross-checks* one source of cues with another
• he *repeats* as if to *confirm* his reading so far
• he *self-corrects* assuming the initiative for making cues match
• he *solves* new words by these means (see also page 62).

Extending these operations

As the child reaches out to more complex texts and writes longer and more involved stories these operations will be used with increasing speed and fluency on

• longer stretches of meaning
• less familiar language
• less predictable texts.

10:   Linking Sound Sequence With Letter Sequence

Introduction

In earlier sections ideas were introduced for developing

A   the analysis of sounds in spoken words (auditory)
and
B   the analysis of signs in written words (visual).

Reading recovery teachers found children who could do **A** but not **B** and vice versa.

They also found children who could do both **A** and **B** as separate activities but who could not link one with the other. The activities listed below were found useful in developing links between *how the child analyses the sounds of words he needs to write or to check in his reading* and *how the child analyses the letters and letter clusters in a word in his reading against the word he is trying to say.*

As we came to understand these problems we learned that this was not a simple problem of phonics. This was an inability to coordinate two complex sets of operations — sound sequence analysis and letter sequence analysis.

In many classrooms around the world while teachers have been teaching phonics competently children have probably been learning something much more useful. They have been constructing the complex associations between sound sequences and letter sequences that enable us to become fluent readers.

We found children who needed extra help to begin to make these links for themselves. Once they understood the nature of the task they began to teach themselves in ways that were more efficient than any instruction programme could hope to be.

If the child can move easily from sounds to letters or from letters to sounds he is easily prompted by the teacher.

Check to see if what you read looks right and sounds right to you. Some children are unable to initiate such checks.

Recovery procedures

If the child finds it hard to go from sounds to letters
In his reading a child may focus on letters and be able to remember the sounds they make and yet that child may find it difficult to go from hearing the sounds in words to producing the letters he needs to represent those sounds in his writing.

Hearing the sounds in words
Get the child to articulate the word he wants to write slowly, pushing counters into boxes in the Elkonin word diagram for each sound he can hear (see page 51). Help him to fill in the boxes.

Make and say
• If the word is a basic sight word, that he cannot yet write, ask him what he would expect to see at the beginning, and/or the end, and/or the middle.
• Give him the correct magnetic letters and ask him to make it on the magnetic board. Make him construct the word several times to get the sequence right.
• Say *'Look at the word. Say it slowly and run your finger across it.'*
• Ask him to close his eyes.
• Ask him to write it without looking.
• Write it several times to get overlearning.

What does he expect to see
• Ask the child to locate a particular interest word in a new reading text *after* he has said what he would expect to see at the beginning.
• Get him to confirm or discount miscues in his reading by covering the problem word and getting him to say what he would expect to see at the beginning, at the end, in the middle and then asking him to check visually. The aim is to get him to engage in independent monitoring of his own attempts and to develop revision through checking.

If the child finds it hard to go from letters to sounds
A child may be able to analyse sounds to letters in his writing and in Elkonin type tasks but may not be able to use letter-to-sound associations to help him eliminate miscues in his reading.

Using his own stories
• Get the child to remake his own stories that have been rewritten on paper strips and cut up. The sounds of the story are in his head and he uses these as a guide to finding the words he has written.
• Ask the child to clap syllables and show you where to cut a word into two parts. Then get him to remake the story.

On books
• When the child comes to a problem word in the text, sound the initial letter for him to help him to predict what the right word might be. Then transfer this sounding task to him by getting him to attend to the initial letter or letters and to get his mouth ready to say it.

The aim is to make him more conscious of a strategy that will help him to eliminate the words that would fit the context but not the first letter cues.

• If he has good mastery of sound-to-letter analysis but

yet does not independently attempt some analysis of simple words in text, write them letter by letter on the blackboard, getting him to articulate the accumulating letters until the word that would fit the context comes into his head — *c   cr   cra   crash.*

Making this operation more explicit

Check on some words accurately read with '*How did you know?*' or '*Were you right?*'

In reading instruction, this invites the child to examine his own behaviour after he has successfully applied the necessary operations to his reading. For example:

The child read *from* as *for* in a sentence and corrected himself.
The teacher asked '*Is it from?*'
The child replied '*It starts with f.*'
The teacher said '*So does for.*'
The child said '*It ends with m.*'

It seems legitimate to encourage a child to verbalize these operations from time to time as a check on what he is doing. Verbalizing is a tactic that could be overworked however, and could interfere with the automatic responding that is required for fluency. (See also page 50.)

11:   Teaching for Word Analysis

Introduction

Most schemes for teaching word analysis begin with the assumptions that

- the teacher needs an instructional sequence
- this can be arrived at by some logical ordering process.

In these reading recovery procedures we have assumed that the goal of tutoring is to achieve the most rapid acceleration possible for the child, and, therefore

- that the child's skills should determine the sequence
- that the word segments attended to should be those used by good readers at this level of learning to read
- that the sequence should be ordered by psychological rather than logical factors.

Following these assumptions and referring to research on early reading and to Elkonin's work we have found that *initial letters* and *final letters* are the starting points for a child's detailed analysis of words and that quite rapidly he goes beyond this to *easy-to-hear consonants within a word, easy-to-hear vowels and other consonants* and *hard-to-hear-vowels.*

If the child is writing stories and doing an Elkonin-type analysis of the new words he wants to write, the problem to be faced by the teaching procedures in this section is — *Does he attempt a left-to-right analysis of new words in his reading?*

But, good readers read in chunks. They attach sounds to a group of letters (rather than each letter) if that works. So the child's attention should be directed to the largest chunks or groups of letters within words that will achieve the analysis. This aim conflicts with many reading programmes which insist on directing the child's attention to the smallest units.

Recovery procedures for word analysis

Initial letter or signs
Draw attention to initial letters:

- Words that begin with the same sound — *Frank, father, Harry, here.*
- Confusable words with different first letters — *smoke, firemen, hose.*
- Go from first letter to sound.
- Go from sound to expected first letter.
- Go from first letter sound to predict the word and say '*What else could you check?*'
- What do initial 'speech marks' tell you.
- Deal with capital/lower case contrasts — *Going, going, Is, is.*

Final letters or signs
Draw attention to final letters:

- The presence of *s* — plural *trees,* possessive *Lizard's,* verb *jumps.*
- The absence of *s.*
- Punctuation — full-stop, questions, exclamations, speech marks.
- Final letters in words — *it, in, his, him, but, bun, bus, buzz.*

First steps in word study

The child has to discover the significant features in a word that will allow him to recognize it another time. Word building or writing can help him do this.

When a child can build a word, slowly but correctly, give him three or more opportunities to

- do it again
- do it more quickly
- do it another way
- do it in another place
- do it fast.

These encourage habituation of the response, overlearning that resists forgetting, automatic responding and flexibility.

- Use magnetic letters for building, dismembering, and reforming words. The actions needed for this help to make many points about letter sequences.
- Use chalk and blackboard for rewriting a word many times.
- Use a larger than usual print with a felt pen.
- Use a paintbrush and water on a blackboard.
- Use written words cut into two or three pieces.
- Use word cards for practice and revision *only after learning has occurred.*

Some distinctions that are needed for early reading books are:

- Between pairs in these groups.

this,	*the*	*that,*	*then*
and,	*am*	*at,*	*a*
me,	*we*	*he,*	*she*

- Between capital and lower case pairs.

Here, here	*In, in*
Is, is	*And, and*

- Between proper names when needed.
Andrew, Ann

- Between confusions as they arise.

Here, the	*a, the*
am, on	*help, play*

- Between words only as needed for the particular texts
shouted/said.

In addition to the necessary distinctions spend some time on word building from the child's repertoire.

baby, bird, bee
struck, duck, luck, muck
cat, can, came
big, bag, bug
fast, first, feast

Preparing for using letter groups or 'chunks' of information
Hearing the breaks: clapping two- and three-syllable words
As opportunities arise with multisyllabic words ask the child to clap the syllables.

jum/bo/jet	*stick/ing*
el/e/phant	*plast/er*
Pe/ter	*hip/po/pot/a/mus*
go/ing	*mo/ther*

Distinguishing similar words.
A Related to a topic.
B With similar components.
Use opportunities as they arise such as

space/man	*up/stairs*
space/ship	*down/stairs*
fire/men	*in/to*
fire/engine	*to/day*

Encourage flexibility in thinking about letters and letter groups in words. Have the child build words from magnetic letters.

Say *'Use two letters to make one word.'*
Or *'Use three letters to make one word.'*
Or *'Use four letters to make one word.'*
Ask *'How many letters are in your word?'*
'Show me a letter. Show me a word.'

Engage in as much word building with magnetic letters as is needed to foster the visual analysis of words in text.
The manipulation in constructing words, in breaking up words, and in substituting letters is important for reading recovery children.

am, Sam, Ham, ham
father, mother, sister, water, her, over
look-s, -ed, -ing
like-s, -ed
play-s, -ed, -ing
go, going
play, please

When the child begins to indicate such analysis for himself during text reading this word building with magnetic letters is only used for a particular teaching point.
The visual analysis of words in text can be encouraged by the teacher's questions as the child reads text.

- After success in word solving.
Say *'How did you know it was...?'*
- When the child stops at a new word.
Say *'What could you try...?'*
Or *'Do you know a word like that?'*
Or *'What would you think it could be?'*
Or *'Do you know a word that starts with those letters?'*
Or *'Do you know something that ends with those letters?'*
Or *'What do you know that might help?'*

An example of fostering the use of letter clusters
The child, reading the word *joking*, stops.
T *'What does it start with?'*
Ch *'j'*
T *'Can you say more than that?'*
Ch *'jo - k ... joke'*
T *'Is the end of joke right?'*
Ch *'ing ... joking'*
T *'Yes. You found two parts to that word, jok and ing. We could look at other words like that*
pok   ing
tak   ing
hik   ing
Let's go on with the story.

Outcome — The value of using letter clusters has been stressed.

The usual analysis of words into useful letter clusters will also be developed in the Writing Stories exercises and associated Elkonin-type analyses. The child will want to hurriedly write down the clusters he knows, resisting a teacher's attempts to get him to work letter by letter. And rightly so.

Teaching and testing for control of letter groups

This is done in a task like the Writing Vocabulary Test. The child is asked to write some words he knows and as opportunities arise he is asked to write another word differing in one letter or letter cluster from the one he has already written. Two or three substitutions of this kind can be asked for.

This is very similar to the word-constructing and letter-substituting tasks he used to do with magnetic letters but it is harder in this 'spelling exercise' form.

12: Teaching for a Sequencing Problem

This may be caused by lack of feeling for direction or by poor checking skills for maintaining consistency. It occurs in children who have some elementary reading skills.

1 Have the child construct a tricky word out of ready-made (magnetic) letters.
   Say *'Once more, as fast as you can,'* encouraging several attempts to provide practice for doing this fluently.
2 Have the child write a word in an unlined book several times. Say *'Once more as fast as you can'*, encouraging correct and fluent performance. Write this word in a sentence in an unlined book.
3 Use word building, word demolition, and reconstruction, making new words with substitution of magnetic letters.
4 Practise word—construction letter by letter on the blackboard in a word diagram. (See sound segmentation page 51.)
   'What can you hear at the beginning?'
   'What can you hear at the end?'

Articulate carefully letter by letter for the child so that you lengthen the particular letter he is working out.

Have the child reconstruct a cut-up child-dictated sentence which the teacher has written. Gradually as the child improves direct his attention to finer detail in the following order:

A Phrasing.
B Words.
C Small segments — obvious syllables, endings, common consonant clusters, vowel-consonant clusters (s - and).

The challenge is to maintain sequence despite the attention to detail.

Have at hand masking cards with windows of various sizes to expose segments or groups of units to be attended to. (This is a visual attending device but can also be used to foster correct sequencing.) Use these on text as the child reads or following a page where a difficulty occurred.

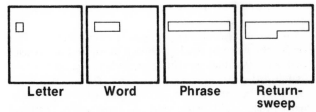

| Letter | Word | Phrase | Return-sweep |

Mask a problem word in text and exposing a sound unit at a time, have the child blend these in the correct sequence.

13: Strong Skills Which Block Learning

Introduction

If some inappropriate reading skill or responses to a particular item become overlearned and fluent they are hard to unlearn. Some guidelines are:

• Prevent the inappropriate behaviour occurring whenever possible.
• Penetrate the old pattern by splitting it apart — over space and over time.
• Use exaggeration by shouting, by stress, by elaborate acting, singing in the manner of recitative, and so on.
• Move with large movements before refining the pattern.
• Aim to get flexibility, and alternative operations established.
• Move cautiously towards fluency. The child may manage to control a new response by thinking about it, and although this makes for slow responding, he may then be able to control the old rapid, unthinking, response.

Sometimes children fail to integrate cues from different sources because they tend to focus on one kind of cue ignoring discrepancies in the other types of cue.

As the child reads, his teacher's confirmation of his successful processing, and the nature of her prompts become important ways of focussing the child's attention on neglected areas.

What is the teacher's purpose in the questions she uses when she prompts? Probably she has several different kinds of prompts. Sometimes she invites the child to think about meaning as in:

Where do you think the bear lives? (Target word: *cave*)

At other times the prompt may be to check something, like a previous sentence or a re-run of the present sentence (perhaps it was sleeping in the ...).

Another kind of leading question may point the reader towards letter/sound cues, like *'What sounds can you see in that word?'* or *'Get your mouth ready for the first sound'.*

And yet another strategy may be to encourage the child to solve the word by analogy with a more frequently used word. This is sometimes difficult, and *cave* is an example of such difficulty.

If a teacher specializes in one type of prompting or cueing the child will tend to specialize (through deprivation of alternative opportunities) and will not achieve flexibility in his use of strategies.

If the child has a bias towards the use of language cues, the teacher's prompts will be directed to either a strong locating response (she may ask him to *'Try that again with your finger')* or to print detail (she may get the child to confirm a prompt by attending to initial and final letters firstly in the spoken word and then in the written word).

14:   When it is Hard to Remember

Introduction

Some children have particular difficulty in calling up an association of a label for a word, or a name for a letter or the names for story characters. I refer here to children who have difficulty with recall on most occasions, not merely a temporary lapse. This low recall means that the earliest, easiest and most basic links of oral language with print are very difficult for the child to establish. Some of the following approaches may help. The teaching goal is to develop strategies for remembering or recalling rather than merely forcing a particular association into the child's mind.

Use the child's association
When Paul knew very few letters he never had difficulty with O.

O for Oboe.

For him that was easy; for another child it would have been impossible.

Mark had trouble with G. After several weeks his teacher found an appropriate meaningful association that triggered the letter name. By calling part of the symbol a saddle she taught Mark to say *'A saddle for the gee-gee'.*

Arrange for repetition
Increase the opportunities to recall, that is to use strategies for remembering, on a few very important items. Practise recall on known items.

Arrange for overlearning
This refers to the practice we get after something has been learned. It is an insurance against forgetting.

Continue to provide opportunities for further practice long after the labels or names seem to have been learned.

Use games
Sometimes a game like *'Snap'*, or matching face-down cards is useful for providing both practice and the expectation that one has to remember.

Revise
Regularly go back to old difficulties and check that they have been established by repetition and overlearning.

Teach for flexibility
Use:
1   different responses like singing, shouting, or role-playing suitable actions, as for oboe, or gee-gee.
2   different mediums such as magnetic letters, chalk, felt-tip pens, paint, cards, slide-projection.

Extend the known set
Have several cards of all the letters/words that the child recognizes plus the ones that are half known plus one or two that have just been taught. Run through these making 'your pile' and 'my pile' of the known and not known words.

Games can be adapted for the purpose of increasing the items that a child remembers. For example, in *'Fishing'*, the teacher makes several cards of each of the words that the child knows with upper and lower case versions. The game is to form pairs by asking your partner if he has a word that you have in your hand.

*'Do you have **go**?'*
'Yes' (He hands it to the teacher) or
'No — Fish' (The teacher picks one from the centre
pile)

Studying words and remembering them

A child may have some reading skill but may show little
skill in accumulating new words or profiting from
instruction given only the day before. It is as if he cannot
'hold' the experience, and store it for future use.

Develop a way of studying words

Help the child to develop a consistent approach to
remembering words. Adapt it to suit the strengths and
weaknesses of each child.

- Ask the child to look at the word written on the
blackboard or with magnetic letters or in large print. Say
it slowly and run your finger across it.
- Ask him to do this.
- Ask him to close his eyes and see it, saying it in parts.
- Ask him to look again, scanning it without help, and
saying it in parts. (The problem is probably that he does
not search with his eyes the letter outlines, or the letter
sequences.)
- Ask him to write it, or parts of it, without looking. (Do
not be too strict on this point for young children.) Have
him say it as he writes it.

   Now present the words in different ways calling for the
same responses from the child.

Practise word reconstruction

- Make the word out of magnetic letters. Jumble and
remake until the child is fluent.
- Write the word on the blackboard in large print using
verbal instructions while writing each letter.

Introduce tracing

If visual analysis and word reconstruction do not produce
good results, introduce tracing and add the feel of the
movements to the child's sources of information.

- Ask the child to trace the word with finger contact
saying the part of the word as he traces it. *Finger contact
is important.*
- Repeat this process as often as is necessary until the
child can write the word without looking at the copy.
- Write the word on scrap paper as often as is needed to
reach fluency.

Other activities

- Encourage the child to include the word in his written
story.
- Choose books that include the new word.

- Establish fluency in producing this vocabulary of
known words.

A way of remembering

When a child has used these rather laborious strategies
for establishing his early visual memories for a small
vocabulary of words he usually arrives at the stage where
he can take short cuts.

'. . . one of the most interesting things to be found in
our non-reading cases (was that) the child, who had to
trace each word many times at first, eventually
developed the ability to glance over the words of four
and five syllables, say them once or twice as he looked
at them and then write them without a copy.'
(Fernald, 1943, pp. 21ff)

   The child is then able to learn from the printed word by
merely looking at it and saying it to himself before he
writes it. He may use one of several strategies — silent
articulation, visual scanning or some other aid.
   Dale was certain about his visual memory for some
words. The teacher said, *'Have a look at "come", a really
good look and then write it down there.'*
   Dale replied, *'I don't have to look.'* He covered his eyes
and wrote the word. But his final comment was
interesting. He said, *'Then you aren't looking and your
eyes help you.'*

Relating new words to old

If something is completely novel it requires a great deal of
effort to learn about it. If we can relate the new item to
something we already know it is easier to master.
   To make the child an independent reader the teacher
must encourage him to search for links between new
words and words he already knows.
   Word construction, demolition and substitution
activities help to build such habits of search.
   Questioning during book reading can also foster a
search for relationships.

15: Teaching for Phrasing and Fluency

Encourage the child to read familiar text quickly. Say
'Can you read this quickly', or *'Put them all together so
that it sounds like talking'.*
   Insist that the child pause appropriately, especially at
full-stops and speech marks. Say *'Read the punctuation.'*
   Read a story to the child; re-read it with the child
emphasizing the phrasing. This should provide support
from the feel and the sound of the patterns of words and
breaks or pauses.

Write down a repetitive sentence or phrase from a specially selected story and treat it like the story described above.

Especially with direct speech ask the child to read it as he would if he was in that situation. For example, *'I'll eat you up.'*

Use known texts, or texts with rhythm-like songs and poems (or sometimes prose) because they carry the reader forward.

Mask the text with a card, or your thumb and expose two or three words at a time asking the child to *'Read it all.'*

Use an overhead projector, masking the text and pacing the child as you expose some for him to read.

Slide a card underneath each line if you wish to discourage word by word reading, finger pointing or voice pointing.

Slide a card over the text forcing the child's pace so he processes a little more fluently without breaking down. This encourages him to make his eyes work ahead of his voice.

Reading Recovery Research Project

A reading recovery programme should be thought of as a second wave of teaching effort. Most children will learn to read in a good class programme that is tuned to individual needs. Twenty percent or more will profit from supplementary and individual tutoring in reading recovery programmes for young children. For a small number who need long-term specialist attention a third wave of effort is required. After three to six months of individual tutoring in a good reading recovery programme the child who has not responded to the programme should be transferred to a trained reading clinician for more specialized help before the end of the second year of instruction.

The reading recovery programme was designed and evaluated as a solution to the institutional problem of how to change the educational system to undercut the incidence of reading failure. While it aims to provide individual help for young children after one year at school it does not preclude the need for, or appropriateness of, even earlier and more specialized intervention for particular children, if this can be made available.

Background to the Project

From 1962 to 1966 in an observational research project the early reading behaviours of 100 New Zealand urban children were recorded at weekly intervals. Out of this work and many workshops and discussions with teachers some materials were published which were designed to help teachers

• understand the reading process
• understand what was happening in New Zealand class-rooms
• become more sensitive observers of their pupils
• diagnose reading difficulties at the end of the first year of instruction.

Although the materials provided the means for detecting early difficulty, no research guidance was available to help teachers work with the children in difficulty. To fill that gap the present project was begun in 1976.*

The Project, 1976-1977

This project set out to explore and describe the range and variability of reading behaviours in children with marked difficulty in beginning reading and who were about 6:0. The children in this programme typically had a year of instruction and frequently seemed to be confused by the reading task, or else they had learned to do inappropriate things, or had a strange view of what reading was about. A few were children of low intelligence and some who required long-term reading clinic tuition were identified.

The project also sought to explore and describe the variability of teaching responses made to these children in individual reading tuition by a group of teachers. It included an in-service training component by involving several tutor-teachers, class teachers, Senior Teachers of Junior Classes, Principals, reading advisers, and parents, all of whom observed some tutoring sessions and discussed child behaviours and teaching strategies. In the first two years of the project videotape demonstrations of reading behaviours before and after tuition and of teaching techniques were made and a draft manual of procedures was written.

Developing the recovery procedures

The difficulties which were demonstrated by the 6-year-old children who were referred to the programme were diverse. No two children had the same problem. Procedures for dealing with these problems were evolved by observing teachers at work, challenging, discussing and consulting in an effort to link teacher and pupil behaviours with theory about the reading process.

A large number of techniques are piloted, observed, discussed, argued over, written up, modified, and related to theories of learning to read. Some were expanded, others were discarded. As a result some carefully graded sequences within each technique were described.

Tutor-teachers were challenged by their colleagues, acting as observers, to explain why they chose a technique, a particular book, or a specific progression. Tutor-teachers were asked

• what contributed to the decision
• how they could justify it

* The Department of Education in Auckland supported this project by paying the salary of a part-time teacher, Susan M. Robinson during 1976-1977 and Barbara Watson in 1978. A research grant from the University of Auckland paid for a research assistant to help with the final testing.

- what other difficulties or achievements the new procedure related to
- why they did not move the child more quickly
- why the child reacted in this or that way.

During such discussions the implicit assumptions of tutor-teachers' decisions were explained verbally rather than remaining intuitive hunches. The process of articulating the basis for a teaching decision was always difficult, and sometimes uncomfortable or embarrassing. The procedures arose from the responses of experienced teachers to children's reading behaviours. The process of evolution and refinement continued over three years and the written accounts of these were edited and revised many times. Many techniques were tried and only the most effective were retained.

Study 1: Teachers with specialist knowledge, 1977

In four teaching terms in 1976 to 1977 six tutor-teachers taught selected children for two 40 minute lessons each week supplementing the group instruction of the classroom with individual tuition. We wanted to capture some of the different approaches that different teachers had to individual children with reading problems. The teachers agreed to teach at least one child, and to meet once a fortnight to observe each other teach and discuss methods and assumptions. This discussion led to further refinement of our teaching procedures.

At this stage we were learning from teachers with experience in teaching children with reading problems. We were not training them in any particular techniques. The progress of the children was not wholly satisfactory but we were only accepting very difficult cases. In our clinical-type programme the experienced teachers tried to use their own procedures to recover children who were already failing and return them to group instruction in classes. This was not an easy task but within one term for many, and two terms for some, some progress was achieved according to our detailed measures for all 30 children tutored in Study 1.

The shifts these children made in book levels indicated only slight progress in many cases. The tutor-teachers found that the child had to be taught many different kinds of behaviours, and helped to read many easy books which provided opportunities to practise those new behaviours.

What happens as children make progress in reading? The child is able to read progressively harder texts and one example of such a gradient of difficulty is provided by the books of a basic reading series. But that is not a good description of what is being learned. How does reading behaviour change as the child reads more diffi-

cult texts? What is happening to the components of the reading process that were measured by selected tests.

To capture shifts in these test scores which might be related to the difficulties of particular children or to the difficulty of the text which the child could attempt, the test scores were reduced to a common normalized scale of Stanine scores (Lyman, 1963). Children on the same level of text varied in their profiles of test scores, and children on texts at different levels of difficulty overlapped in their range of test scores. The suitability of the text was being carefully selected and monitored by tutors to have the children reading above 90 percent difficulty level at all times. One may conclude therefore that these children read texts of similar difficulty with skills of different strengths. It follows from this that each child's reading recovery programme was designed to suit the low skills in his repertoire and so programmes differed from child to child. This assumes that the behaviours being measured are critical for progress in the New Zealand programme.

A follow-up check on two-thirds of these children in 1978, seven to eleven months after tutoring finished showed

- that the children who went furthest in the programme maintained their progress in the classroom.
- that the lowest-scoring children at the end of tutoring had made minimal progress in their classrooms: children at the Red and Yellow Book Level of the *Ready to Read* series did not progress in their J2 classes.

The four most important implications for the next stage of our project were thought to be these.

1 Children probably need an *intensive* programme to gain satisfactory reading skills. These children had only two supplementary lessons a week.
2 The best teaching procedures from our pooled resources should be gathered together and articulated to provide better guidance for tutors.
3 The goal of teaching should be a self-improving system, a set of behaviours which, merely because the child practises them lead to control over more difficult texts. Important components of a self-improving system are the strategies or operations which allow the child to detect that an error had been made and to find some way of righting the wrong. Teachers in the next study would need to deliberately focus the child's attention on such operations.
4 We must think clearly about the process and implications of discontinuing children from tutoring and ensuring an effective transfer back to class programmes with continuing progress.

The Field Trials, 1978

If a preventive programme were to be adopted in New Zealand schools on a large scale we would need to demonstrate that our procedures could work in the practical school setting. The task for the programme in 1978 was to introduce reading recovery programmes in five schools that were very different in order to discover

• what difficulties would be encountered in a school setting
• what different solutions to organization and procedure were necessary in different settings
• more about how the programme would be used by different teachers for whom the procedures were novel.

Research questions

We asked —

1   How was the programme implemented?

   • Could teachers without specialist training or university study use the procedures effectively?
   • How would the programmes need to vary from school to school?

2   What reading progress was made?

   • To what extent could the poorest readers be helped by individual tutoring?
   • How many could be helped?
   • What were the outcomes of the programme for the tutored children in comparison with the untutored?
   • Could the gains made in tutoring be sustained after withdrawal of the supplementary tutoring?

If a fixed plan of operation had been laid out there would have been no room for the individual differences that should occur because teachers differ, schools differ, and children in different schools differ. How teachers worked, how many children they took each day or week and what timetables they derived were not set by this project. Teachers discussed their ideas on these matters with the Research Coordinator, the Research Director and/or the other teachers. Consultation was the keyword. We did not want to prescribe how the teachers should operate the scheme. (For details of how we introduced the procedures to teachers see the tutoring programme on page 70.)

The schools

The schools were chosen because of differences in size, type of organization*, population and location. All were in the suburbs of a large metropolitan area. School A was a small school in an older state housing area with some solo parents. School B was in a mixed working and middle class suburb. School C was on the edge of both a middle class and a working class new housing area. It was the biggest school. In School D the children were predominantly from working class backgrounds with a high proportion of Maori and Island children and much movement in and out of the school. School E was a larger school in a newer state housing area with 60 percent of the children having solo parents.

The teachers

Principals in those five schools were asked to use the Year-four teacher allocated as an extra teacher and for this project, to release a more experienced volunteer teacher for full-time teaching on a one-to-one basis in the reading recovery programme. The teachers released had 5, 6, 9, 12, and 12 years experience. The sum total of their university training was two papers in Education. The conditions of the school's participation in the study were

• that the teacher be allowed to test every 6-year-old within two weeks of his/her birthday.
• that she arrange a programme of individual and/or small group tutoring.
• that this programme would not be interrupted for any reasons such as relieving, sports duties and school trips.

The reasons for the special conditions were that in this field trial research project the practical usefulness of the procedures were being put to the test and other distractors which could reduce the effectiveness of the programme had to be minimized.

Testing all children at 6:0

The total age cohort was tested in the schools and included all children whose birthdays fell between 1 September, 1977 and 30 September 1978. The dates of testing, linked to sixth birthdays, were scattered throughout the year. The mean age of the 291 children at initial testing was 6 years 1.5 months (S.D. 2.14 months). Because testing began in February 1978 but included children born in September, children were tested when they moved into the schools later in the school year if they belonged to the same age cohort.

The five teachers were trained to administer the tests of the Diagnostic Survey and to write a Diagnostic Summary Report which analysed the child's useful reading strategies on text, on words, and on letters, and

*Two schools had open plan or open space junior departments.

similarly the child's problem strategies on *each* of the above.

Who was tutored?

From the 291 children who met the age criteria and who had already been in a reading instruction programme for one year, a group of 122 children were given special help. Then, in the last two months of 1978, 282 children or 96.5 percent of the age group were retested.* Only nine children who had moved away from Auckland could not be traced, one from the programme and eight from the non-tutored group. At this time the mean age was 6 years 7.5 months (S.D. 3.8 months).

Children had progressed at very different rates in their first year at school. How children were distributed throughout the reading books differed markedly from school to school. There were two main reasons for this. One was that the children entering the schools differed in background experience and ability from school to school. The other was that each school paced the introduction of the reading programme differently.

Some schools began book reading early and pushed ahead rather rapidly. Others took a longer time to establish foundation skills.

Children selected for individual tutoring were not chosen by setting a particular attainment level. *They were the lowest scorers on text reading in that particular school.* The lowest scorers in School C might be better than some of the higher scorers in School E. It was not the point of this study to raise all children's performance above a particular level. A teacher was available in each school and she was trying to raise the peformance of the low progress readers *in that school.*

The number (and the proportion of the age-cohort) who were individually tutored differed from school to school because of the school's size and because of the variations in the needs of the children. The working week of the teacher set limits on how many children were in her programme. The responsiveness of children to individual teaching determined the time allocated for lessons and the weeks the child remained in the study. Factors which tended to lengthen time in the programme were language problems, family mobility, unsettled family circumstances, sickness and/or absence, general retardation, and unusual learning problems.

Two groups of children were admitted to individual teaching. The first group had learned very little about reading and after more than 12 months at school were still at a Caption, Red or Yellow book level.* The second group we called 'gap-fillers'. They were children, able to read Blue to Green level books who had low scores on one or more of the tests. Assuming that the tests evaluated progress in essential components of the reading process (and we did assume this) then these were children with gaps in their reading behaviours. Initially these children provided a wider range of problems for the teachers to train on, but they tended to make rapid progress and leave the programme after about six weeks.

Before they began tutoring, teachers wrote out predictions of what changes they would expect to see in the reading behaviours of the children as they improved. This helped them to specify the programme goals for each child individually.

The tutoring programme

The teaching was done in an individual programme supplementing the work of the classroom.

The Diagnostic Summary Report gave the teacher an analysis of behaviours that should relate directly to her teaching programme. She arranged to see children on any timetable that suited her and the school. Sometimes this was once a day (30 to 45 minutes) and sometimes twice a day for two sessions of 30 and 10 minutes (see Table 1). Occasionally towards the end of their programme children would come to her in twos and threes but most of the instruction was individual.

A typical tutoring session included each of these activities in this order

- re-reading of two or more familiar books — *text*
- letter identification — *letters*
(plastic letters on a magnetic board)
- writing a story — *text*
- sound analysis of words — *sounds*
(Elkonin technique)
- cut-up story to be rearranged — *text*
- new book introduced — *text*
- new book attempted — *text*

The bias towards using text for most of the work was deliberate. As the goal of the programme was to return children to existing reading groups in their classrooms it was necessary to accelerate their progress to achieve this. Accelerated progress would be most likely to be achieved if:

- the child had many opportunities to practise.

---

*All children who had moved to other schools in Auckland, 17 untutored children and 10 tutored children were retested in this group.

*The *Ready to Read* Series, Department of Education, Wellington, 1963.

• the task was the same as the one on which improvement was required.
• the child was building a complex, flexible system of alternative responses (Clay, 1979).*

If skills are taught in isolation more time must be spent in learning to combine these, and more difficulty is experienced with switching to alternative responses.

Teachers were encouraged to draw on their own experience at first. Gradually the procedures outlined in the working manual of reading recovery procedures were introduced and demonstrated, and teachers were encouraged to change their concept of the task. Every two weeks one of the five teachers would demonstrate by teaching one of her pupils while the other teachers observed and discussed the procedures on the other side of a one-way screen.

The teacher's manual, a draft of the procedures that could be used, was not yet as clear as we would want it to be. The project teachers were asked to help us improve the manual, making the messages clearer and more directly applicable to the problems they, the teachers, encountered. The manual did not provide a simple set of instructions that could be read and then implemented, but it was a reference source, and a basis for discussion and clarification of concepts. When teachers found the manual unclear they would discuss the problem with the Research Coordinator during her fortnightly visit to the school or with the group of teachers at the fortnightly demonstration and discussion sessions at the university. The manual was used, and criticized. The hundreds of pencilled comments on the master copy which led to the final revision of the procedures at the end of the year, attested to this.

Topics raised by the teachers in these discussions seemed to suggest that their attention to the reading process was shifting

*We have been criticized for forcing children who would learn if they were allowed to come in their own time. There are four main arguments against this position. Firstly a child who gets further and further out of step with the system, loses his opportunity to learn from it, if only because a system providing for numbers of children cannot be infinitely variable to suit individuals. Secondly, as soon as a child can *read to learn* he has a powerful new means of enriching his own education: it is not essential for education but it is means by which one can become better educated. Thirdly, a long delay in reaching success in reading carries high risks to emotional development and one's self-concept. Fourthly, we have watched particular children in our research records habituate inappropriate responding. This creates an almost impenetrable barrier to subsequent satisfactory progress.

• from teaching for items of knowledge (letters known, words remembered) and from getting the child to habituate a skill or memorize a new element
• to developing in the child the confidence and willingness to use a variety of strategies.

Another feature of the shift was away from having the 'poor reader' dependent on the teacher and towards teaching in such a way that the child had many opportunities to teach himself something.

Records

Teachers were encouraged to keep an unstructured diary or log book as a personal history of the year's work. Personal reactions and queries were to be dated and entered on both teacher behaviours and perceptions, and child behaviours.

• A Diagnostic Summary Report was prepared for each child when he was accepted into the project.
• Either a Lesson Plan or a Lesson Summary was kept for each session with the child, detailing at what point in the teaching sequences the teacher was working and how the child responded. This provided a record of the small step gains made by each child, and of the progressions which the teacher selected from the manual.
• One Running Record of text reading was usually kept for each session.
• A graph of progress by Book Level was plotted from one Running Record each week.

Contact with parents

This was left to the teacher and Principal. In 1976 to 1977 we had close contact with the parents of the children on the project. At the fortnightly demonstration sessions it was not unusual for parents to join with teachers in watching on one side of the one-way screen. This provided the Research Director with opportunities for discussing aspects of the child's progress with parents.

We hoped schools would feel free to approach parents in whatever would be their normal procedure. In fact, contacts were minimal.

Discontinuing tutoring

When the tutor-teachers judged from the children's work that they would be able to work with and survive in an appropriate group in their classroom and maintain their progress they recommended the child for discontinuing.

At this point an independent tester re-administered the Diagnostic Survey to provide an objective check on the teacher's estimate of progress. In most cases when a comparison was made with the entry test scores, progress in all tests was noted and individual tutoring was discontinued. Sometimes a recommendation was made to continue intermittent lessons to support a child or give further instruction in specific areas of weakness. Occasionally a child was not ready to be discontinued. In most cases the teachers had carried the children for longer and to higher levels than we had expected. They were conservative in their recommendations for discontinuing.

New children entered individual tutoring as others were discontinued.

Testing at the end of 1978

In the last two months of 1978 all 282 children (i.e. the age cohort in five schools) were re-tested by two independent testers not the teachers.

Book Level and Reading Vocabulary were the measures of reading progress and testing procedures were followed.

1   Book Level
The most relevant measure for demonstrating progress was Book Level because it assessed the child's ability to use a sequence of cues in a text. A scale of difficulty was provided by two Caption Book steps, 24 steps for the basic reading series plus three paragraphs (2, 3 and 4) from the Neale Analysis of Reading Ability, making 29 steps. The highest level on the scale that a child could attempt with 90 percent (or above) accuracy determined his score. This type of measure has proved a valid and reliable test of reading progress in other research (Clay, 1966; Robinson, 1973; Wade, 1978). It is not an equal interval scale.

2   Reading Vocabulary
A standardized test approach was also used. Previous research with children of this age in New Zealand schools (Clay, 1966) had shown that low progress children could be given the Word Test and high progress children could be given the Schonell R1 test and that a satisfactory measure *for research purposes* was obtained by combining these two scores. This procedure was used again in this study and the combined scores for Reading Vocabulary yielded a normal distribution. A Word Test score provides only a sign or indicator of reading progress, because the test behaviour that is scored does not involve management of the behaviours needed to read continuous text.

The other tests used were:

Concepts About Print (CAP)
Letter Identification (LI)
Writing Vocabulary (WV)
Dictation Test (DIC)

Scores on these tests were interpreted as indicators of necessary component reading skills covering directional and visual discrimination learning (CAP), letter identity (LI), words known in every detail (WV) and sound-to-letter association (DIC).

The 122 children who had been given some individual teaching were classified into three sub-groups at the end of the field trial year:

D — The discontinued and followed-up children who had been recommended and approved for discontinuing and who had been surviving for an average of 12 weeks in their classroom without further help (N=53).
Dd — Children who were still receiving tuition at a time of retesting and whose teacher and tester agreed that they met the criteria used to discontinue children in the D group (N=27).
P — Programme children who were still receiving tuition at the time of retesting, and who needed further help. Most of these children had had shorter periods of tuition (N=42).
Other — There were 160 other children in the age cohort who were tested and did not receive attention.

Preliminary analyses showed that the results for the D and Dd children were very similar and these were then combined leaving a comparison of gains on text reading and component reading test scores between three groups.

Discontinued	(80)
In Programme	(42)
Other Children	(160)

The research questions

The main questions asked in this research project were

1   Can these procedures be introduced with success to schools of different size, and different characteristics? How will teachers adapt this opportunity for individual instruction to the setting of their particular school? What organizational differences will be necessary? Time in programme, numbers of children taught, scheduling of lessons may need to differ.

2   If teachers find the procedures workable then what progress is made?
How is the achievement of the children best described?
a) Not improved — no significant change in level of performance.
b) Improved — gains are less than those predicted for total group.
c) Improved — gains are equal to those predicted for the total group.
d) Accelerated progress — gains are significantly higher than those predicted for the total group.

3   What are the implications of the results for the education system?

Organization Differences in Five Schools

	Number of children in tuition	% of the age cohort	Mean Weeks in Programme[3]			Mean length of lessons (in minutes)	Mean number of lessons
			Discontinued and followed-up	In Programme	Discontinued and not followed-up		
A[1]	22	62	13.8	12.0	16.3	40.5	27.6
B[2]	28	43	11.4	11.8	11.2	40.0	21.8
C	22	29	13.4	13.0	9.7	35.9	33.8
D	29	51	14.6	13.8	11.8	26.7[3]	33.3
E[1,2]	21	40	13.1	15.1	19.2	40.0	26.4
Average		49	14.3	13.1	13.6		

[1] These schools had women principals, the others had men.
[2] These schools had open plan or open space organization for junior classes.
[3] Mean length of lesson affected by some use of group instruction.

Table 1

TABLE A : PROGRESS OF DISCONTINUED CHILDREN IN PROGRAMME (P) AND AT THE END OF 1978 (A)

Child	Sex	Age at Entry to the Programme	Weeks in Tutoring	Number of Tutoring Sessions	Entry to Programme	End of Programme	In Programme Gain in Book Steps (P)	In Programme Gain in Stanine Scores (P)	After Programme Gain in Book Steps (A)	After Programme Gain in Stanine Scores (A)	Total Reading Vocab. P	Total Reading Vocab. A	Word Test P	Word Test A	Schonell R1 P	Schonell R1 A	Concepts About Print P	Concepts About Print A	Letter Identif. P	Letter Identif. A	Writing Vocab. P	Writing Vocab. A	Dictation P	Dictation A
RO	M	6.3	8	30	Caption B	Green 1	10	3	2	0	2	1	2	3	2	1	1	2	1	0	3	0	2	1
RS	M	6.1	9	11	Red 1	Donkeys Egg 1	16	4	3	1	3	1	2	2	3	1	3	0	0	0	4	2	2	0
AW	M	6.2	13	19	Red 1	Hungry Lambs 2	13	3	5	1	2	2	3	0	1	2	3	2	2	0	3	2	3	0
AB	M	6.5	15	19	Red 1	Green 1	9	3	5	1	1	3	1	3	0	2	2	0	2	1	2	2	2	2
CG	F	6.2	**24	36	Red 1	Green 1	9	3	5	1	1	1	0	2	1	1	1	1	1	1	3	2	1	1
LG	F	6.2	13	33	Red 1	Hungry Lambs 2	13	3	5	1	3	1	3	2	3	1	2	2	2	1	2	2	3	1
TS	F	6.3	17	26	Red 1	Hungry Lambs 1	12	3	2	1	2	1	2	3	2	0	4	0	5	-2	3	1	3	0
RH	F	6.2	17	*67	Red 1	Hungry Lambs 2	13	3	2	1	3	0	6	0	1	0	3	0	3	-1	3	2	3	0
RC	F	6.2	19	41	Red 1	Hungry Lambs 1	12	3	3	1	3	1	4	0	2	1	5	1	3	1	2	0	3	0
TK	F	6.3	**31	*89	Red 1	Blue 3	8	3	8	1	3	1	4	2	1	1	2	1	3	3	2	3	4	0
RS	F	6.3	9	17	Red 1	Green 1	9	3	4	0	2	1	3	0	2	1	0	2	2	0	3	2	2	2
TS	F	6.2	23	19	Red 1	Donkeys Egg 1	16	4	1	0	3	0	4	0	3	0	0	1	2	1	3	2	5	0
MP	F	6.0	7	10	Red 2	Hungry Lamba 1	11	2	2	1	2	1	2	2	2	1	2	3	2	0	3	2	-1	0
JL	F	6.5	**33	60	Red 2	Boat Day 1	13	3	5	1	2	1	4	-2	3	1	1	4	4	2	4	1	4	1
PH	M	6.5	**32	45	Red 2	Green 1	8	2	3	0	1	1	1	1	2	0	4	0	3	2	2	1	1	1
TS	M	6.5	18	*27	Red 3	Green 1	7	2	3	0	2	1	1	1	2	1	5	2	1	1	3	1	2	1
MO	F	6.6	15	18	Red 3	Boat Day 1	12	3	4	0	1	1	2	2	1	1	4	2	4	-2	2	3	2	1
SM	F	6.2	17	*38	Yellow 1	Donkeys Egg 2	14	3	2	1	4	1	4	0	2	1	0	3	2	1	4	0	2	1
DX	M	6.0	10	18	Yellow 1	Boat Day 1	11	3	1	0	2	0	3	0	2	1	2	2	2	0	3	1	2	-1
MS	M	6.1	7	9	Yellow 1	Boat Day 1	11	3	1	0	3	-1	4	-2	3	-1	1	0	3	0	3	1	3	0
VP	F	6.3	10	*16	Yellow 1	Boat Day 1	11	3	2	0	1	2	3	0	0	1	-1	0	-1	4	3	2	1	0

(Cont.)

Child	Sex	Age at Entry to the Programme	Weeks in Tutoring	Number of Tutoring Sessions	Entry to Programme	End of Programme	In Programme Gain in Book Steps (P)	In Programme Gain in Stanine Scores (P)	After Programme Gain in Book Steps (A)	After Programme Gain in Stanine Scores (A)	Total Reading Vocab. P	Total Reading Vocab. A	Gain in Word Test P	Gain in Word Test A	Schonell R1 P	Schonell R1 A	Concepts About Print P	Concepts About Print A	Letter Identif. P	Letter Identif. A	Writing Vocab. P	Writing Vocab. A	Dictation P	Dictation A
AP	M	6.2	**17	*45	Yellow 1	Green 1	6	2	5	1	2	1	1	2	2	0	0	1	0	1	1	3	-1	0
NE	F	6.7	11	*11	Yellow 2	Hungry Lambs 1	8	1	2	1	2	1	1	2	2	1	1	1	1	0	4	1	3	1
SR	M	6.0	**17	*19	Yellow 2	Green 1	5	1	4	0	1	1	0	3	1	0	1	3	1	1	1	2	1	1
TF	M	6.1	**15	*20	Yellow 2	Green 1	5	1	4	0	2	1	1	0	2	1	2	-2	1	2	2	1	1	1
NT	M	6.0	10	16	Yellow 3	Donkeys Egg 1	11	2	3	1	2	1	3	0	2	1	2	1	-1	2	4	0	2	1
TA	M	6.7	6	9	Yellow 3	Hungry Lambs 2	8	1	6	2	2	1	1	3	1	1	0	0	1	0	3	2	2	1
LM	M	6.1	11	14	Yellow 3	Donkeys Egg 1	11	2	3	1	2	1	2	2	1	1	2	0	1	0	3	1	2	1
CM	M	6.3	**18	* 9	Yellow 3	Hungry Lambs 1	7	1	4	1	1	3	1	3	2	1	2	-1	0	0	1	2	2	0
CW	F	6.0	**16	*18	Blue 1	Green 3	5	1	4	1	2	1	0	2	2	1	2	3	1	1	2	3	2	2
VN	M	6.2	5	* 7	Blue 1	Hungry Lambs 2	7	1	4	1	1	1	3	0	2	1	1	2	0	1	3	2	0	2
PA	M	6.5	20	*27	Blue 1	Boat Day 2	9	2	1	0	2	1	2	0	1	1	1	2	2	0	3	2	3	0
PM	M	6.0	13	25	Blue 2	Sweet Porridge 1	11	2	2	1	2	1	3	0	1	1	1	0	3	2	3	0	2	0
NR	F	6.3	9	8	Blue 2	Sweet Porridge 2	12	3	3	1	3	1	4	0	2	1	1	1	2	0	4	3	3	0
EH	M	6.2	16	32	Blue 2	Boat Day 1	7	2	5	1	0	1	0	0	1	1	3	0	2	1	4	1	3	0
SR	F	6.4	16	32	Blue 2	Donkeys Egg 1	9	2	3	1	1	1	2	0	1	1	4	0	3	3	4	2	2	1
RA	M	6.0	16	24	Blue 2	Donkeys Egg 1	9	2	3	1	1	1	1	2	0	1	4	1	2	0	3	2	2	1
JS	F	6.1	19	33	Blue 2	Donkeys Egg 1	9	2	3	1	1	1	2	0	1	1	4	0	3	2	3	2	2	1
TB	F	6.5	10	* 5	Blue 3	Hungry Lambs 1	4	0	8	2	1	2	3	0	2	2	2	2	2	0	4	4	3	1
EW	F	6.9	5	* 6	Green 1	Sweet Porridge 1	9	1	5	2	2	0	0	2	1	1	1	0	3	-3	6	2	2	1
KS	M	6.6	9	10	Green 1	Hungry Lambs 1	3	0	2	1	1	1	0	2	1	0	3	2	1	0	2	2	2	-1
DC	F	6.7	**17	24	Green 1	Green 3	2	0	5	1	1	1	1	2	1	1	0	1	2	0	2	2	2	2

(Cont.)

Child	Sex	Age at Entry to the Programme	Weeks in Tutoring	Number of Tutoring Sessions	Entry to Programme	End of Programme	In Programme Gain in Book Steps P	Gain in Stanine Scores P	After Programme Gain in Book Steps A	Gain in Stanine Scores A	Total Reading Vocab. P	A	Word Test P	A	Schonell R1 P	A	Concepts About Print P	A	Letter Identif. P	A	Writing Vocab. P	A	Dictation P	A
KC	F	6.3	4	*3	Green 2	Hungry Lambs 1	2	0	7	2	2	1	1	2	1	1	1	2	0	1	2	2	2	1
CF	F	6.1	14	23	Green 3	Donkeys Egg 1	8	1	2	0	1	1	2	0	1	1	5	-2	4	0	3	0	1	1
GW	M	6.8	**7	*6	Hungry Lambs 1	Donkeys Egg 1	4	1	3	1	2	1	3	0	1	2	2	2	1	1	3	2	0	1
JL	F	6.8	**13	*16	Hungry Lambs 2	Boat Day 2	2	1	4	1	1	2	1	3	0	1	1	2	0	3	1	4	0	0
ZS	M	6.1	7	10	Boat Day 1	Stars in the Sky 1	6	1	4	2	1	1	0	1	2	1	2	1	0	0	2	2	2	0
PD	M	6.7	6	11	Boat Day 2	Sweet Porridge 1	3	0	4	2	1	2	2	0	1	2	2	2	1	0	0	3	2	1
AL	M	6.3	6	9	Boat Day 2	Sweet Porridge 2	4	1	0	0	0	1	0	0	1	1	1	2	1	2	5	-1	2	0
CHILDREN WHO LEFT THEIR SCHOOLS AFTER THE END OF PROGRAMME																								
AH	F	6.1	13	16	Red 1	Donkeys Egg 1	16	4	4	1	3	1	5	0	3	2	4	0	5	0	3	3	3	1
KM	F	6.3	13	*27	Red 2	Donkeys Eggs 1	-15	3	4	1	3	2	4	0	3	3	1	2	2	0	4	2	4	0
LF	F	6.6	12	*17	Blue 3	Hungry Lambs 1	4	0	5	1	2	1	1	0	2	1	2	1	1	1	2	4	3	0
KO	F	6.2	10	17	Blue 3	Sweet Porridge 1	10	1	2	1	2	1	3	2	3	2	2	1	1	2	4	0	3	0

* Session time averaged to 40 minutes.
** Observation time included

TABLE B : PROGRESS OF CHILDREN DISCONTINUED AT THE END OF 1978

Child	Sex	Age at Entry to the Programme	Weeks in Tutoring	Number of Tutoring Sessions	Entry to Programme	End of Year	Gain in Book Steps	Gain in Stanine Scores	Total Reading Vocab.	Word Test	Schonell R1	Concepts About Print	Letter Identif.	Writing Vocab.	Dictation
PH	M	6.5	26	42	Caption A	Green 1	11	4	3	4	2	4	2	2	4
MC	M	6.2	30	68	Caption B	Hungry Lambs 1	13	3	4	3	3	6	3	4	4
AM	M	6.7	19	46	Caption B	Green 1	10	3	4	3	3	3	2	2	2
JM	M	6.3	15	31	Red 1	Boat Day 1	14	4	2	4	2	2	3	4	4
JP	M	6.0	10	21	Red 1	Hungry Lambs 1	12	3	2	4	2	4	3	4	4
MW	F	6.2	22	50	Red 1	Green 2	10	3	2	3	2	5	2	4	5
PH	M	6.2	14	*15	Red 2	Green 2	9	3	2	2	2	2	1	3	2
NT	F	6.0	14	*19	Red 2	Blue 1	5	2	1	1	1	2	2	2	2
PL	M	6.7	15	*27	Red 2	Blue 3	7	2	1	3	1	2	2	3	3
BW	M	6.1	15	24	Red 2	Hungry Lambs 2	12	2	2	3	2	0	3	4	2
DP	M	6.0	14	*62	Red 3	Hungry Lambs 1	10	2	2	4	1	2	1	2	0
GB	M	6.0	8	16	Red 3	Green 1	7	2	1	2	1	2	1	2	2
RC	F	6.7	28	39	Yellow 1	Boat Day 2	12	3	2	2	2	0	2	2	4
KK	M	6.7	12	29	Yellow 2	Hungry Lambs 2	9	1	1	3	0	2	-3	2	1
PC	M	6.0	17	33	Yellow 2	Hungry Lambs 1	8	1	3	3	3	3	2	3	3
GB	M	6.0	17	33	Yellow 2	Green 1	5	1	1	4	0	2	1	3	2
AH	M	6.1	11	20	Yellow 3	Boat Day 1	9	2	3	3	3	1	1	3	2
DT	F	6.0	19	36	Yellow 3	Sweet Porridge 1	11	2	3	4	3	4	2	5	3
CL	M	6.3	12	26	Yellow 3	Hungry Lambs 1	8	1	1	1	1	0	2	4	2
MB	F	6.0	15	28	Blue 1	Green 1	3	1	2	2	2	3	2	5	2
IL	M	6.0	7	17	Blue 2	Hungry Lambs 2	9	1	1	3	1	2	1	3	1
AR	M	6.1	14	22	Blue 2	Stars in Sky 2	14	3	3	2	4	6	2	5	3
JB	M	6.5	4	6	Green 1	Hungry Lambs 2	4	0	2	0	1	1	1	4	.2
KR	M	6.5	4	7	Green 1	Boat Day 1	5	1	1	0	2	3	2	4	1
NJ	F	6.5	3	6	Green 2	Boat Day 1	4	1	0	0	0	-1	0	3	-2

CHILDREN WHO LEFT THEIR SCHOOLS WHILE STILL IN PROGRAMME

Child	Sex	Age at Entry to the Programme	Weeks in Tutoring	Number of Tutoring Sessions	Entry to Programme	End of Year	Gain in Book Steps	Gain in Stanine Scores	Total Reading Vocab.	Word Test	Schonell R1	Concepts About Print	Letter Identif.	Writing Vocab.	Dictation
TM	M	6.1	7	*15	Red 1	Green 1	9	3	3	3	3	2	4	3	2
WP	M	6.3	9	*12	Yellow 3	Boat Day 1	9	2	2	3	2	2	3	5	3

* Session time averaged to 40 minutes.

TABLE C : PROGRESS OF CHILDREN REMAINING IN THE PROGRAMME AT THE END OF 1978

Child	Sex	Age at Entry to the Programme	Weeks in Tutoring	Number of Tutoring Sessions	Entry to Programme	End of Year	Gain in Book Steps	Gain in Stanine Scores	TESTS — Gain in Stanine Scores						
									Total Reading Vocab.	Word Test	Schonell R1	Concepts About Print	Letter Identif.	Writing Vocab.	Dictation
DP	M	6.1	30	* 59	Caption A	Blue 1	8	3	3	2	2	4	2	3	3
JR	M	6.0	8	* 15	Caption A	Yellow 1	5	2	1	1	1	2	2	1	3
DP	M	6.0	18	* 35	Caption A	Red 1	2	1	0	0	0	2	0	0	2
DT	F	6.9	9	* 12	Caption A	Red 1	2	1	2	2	1	2	1	0	3
JP	F	6.1	9	* 18	Caption A	Red 1	2	1	2	1	1	2	0	0	2
CJ	M	6.8	15	* 25	Caption A	Yellow 1	5	2	1	1	1	2	2	1	1
RH	M	6.1	22	* 44	Caption A	Blue 2	9	3	1	3	1	2	2	2	2
JW	M	6.0	12	24	Caption A	Yellow 3	7	3	2	3	2	4	1	2	3
MW	M	6.0	15	* 92	Caption A	Red 1	2	1	0	0	0	2	1	0	1
TS	M	6.5	34	57	Caption A	Blue 2	9	3	2	2	2	2	3	1	2
TC	M	6.1	9	23	Caption A	Yellow 3	7	3	3	3	2	3	2	4	3
KC	F	6.0	11	29	Caption B	Yellow 2	5	2	3	3	1	2	3	3	2
TT	M	6.4	18	22	Caption B	Blue 1	7	2	1	3	1	2	2	2	3
JF	M	6.2	8	24	Caption B	Blue 1	7	2	2	3	2	4	2	2	2
VF	M	6.1	19	* 86	Caption B	Blue 3	9	3	2	3	1	3	2	2	3
JT	F	6.0	10	27	Caption B	Yellow 3	6	2	1	3	1	3	2	4	3
SH	F	6.0	9	19	Caption B	Blue 3	9	3	2	2	1	2	1	5	3
LK	F	6.1	15	31	Caption B	Blue 1	7	2	3	3	2	4	1	3	3
AK	F	6.0	15	27	Caption B	Yellow 3	6	2	3	4	2	3	2	2	3
MW	M	6.1	13	26	Caption B	Yellow 2	5	2	2	3	2	3	1	3	3
PT	M	6.0	9	9	Red 1	Blue 1	6	2	1	2	1	1	2	2	2
RH	M	6.4	33	56	Red 1	Blue 3	8	2	1	3	1	2	3	2	2
DH	M	6.1	9	8	Red 1	Yellow 2	4	2	0	2	0	2	1	2	2
JH	M	6.0	6	16	Red 1	Yellow 1	3	1	1	1	1	2	2	1	2
HP	F	6.3	11	* 16	Red 1	Blue 2	7	2	1	2	1	2	2	2	1
TW	F	6.4	7	* 13	Red 1	Yellow 1	3	1	2	2	2	1	1	3	2
LH	F	6.0	9	* 15	Red 1	Yellow 1	3	1	1	2	1	2	2	2	2
GP	M	6.0	11	* 20	Red 2	Yellow 1	2	0	1	1	1	2	2	1	2
PD	M	6.0	16	23	Red 2	Blue 3	7	2	1	2	1	2	2	1	2
SF	M	6.1	10	37	Red 2	Blue 1	5	1	2	1	2	3	2	2	2
BA	M	6.0	10	* 41	Red 2	Green 1	8	2	0	2	0	0	1	2	1
KP	M	6.5	34	* 54	Red 2	Yellow 1	2	0	1	2	1	2	2	2	2

(cont.)

| | Gain in Stanine Scores | | | | | | | | | | | Book Levels | | | |
Total Reading Vocab.	Word Test	Schonell R1	Concepts About Print	Letter Identif.	Writing Vocab.	Dictation	Child	Sex	Age at Entry to the Programme	Weeks in Tutoring	Number of Tutoring Sessions	Entry to Programme	End of Year	Gain in Book Steps	Gain in Stanine Scores
1	2	1	1	2	3	2	NB	M	6.0	12	45	Red 3	Green 1	7	2
1	3	0	1	2	2	2	AL	F	6.6	8	* 13	Red 3	Yellow 3	3	1
2	2	3	3	3	2	3	DB	M	6.1	14	35	Yellow 1	Green 1	6	2
2	4	2	1	1	4	0	EC	F	6.0	11	* 50	Yellow 1	Green 1	6	2
1	1	1	1	1	3	1	AW	F	6.0	10	* 12	Yellow 2	Blue 2	3	0
2	4	2	2	0	3	0	NM	M	6.0	11	* 38	Yellow 2	Green 3	7	1
							CHILDREN WHO LEFT THEIR SCHOOLS WHILE STILL IN PROGRAMME								
2	3	2	2	2	2	3	JR	M	6.2	8	* 18	Caption A	Blue 2	9	3
1	1	0	2	1	0	1	PC	F	6.5	20	* 41	Caption A	Red 1	2	1
3	4	2	3	3	2	3	KC	M	6.4	5	* 8	Red 1	Yellow 3	5	2
1	2	1	1	0	1	1	DW	M	6.6	3	3	Red 3	Yellow 3	3	1

* Session time averaged to 40 minutes.

Organizational factors

Numbers
The number of children who received tuition ranged from 20 to 30 per teacher and this represented between 29 and 62 percent of the age cohort, depending upon the size of the school. This is shown in Table 1.

Sex of children
61 percent of the children tutored were boys and 39 percent were girls.

Weeks in programme
Table 1 shows the average pattern, and individual school averages, for time in tuition. There was an average lag of three to five weeks between sixth birthday and entry to the programme, for a variety of unavoidable reasons such as vacations, a full tutoring roll, a need for testing to be scheduled and/or absences.

Most children needed about a term of individual tuition to meet the criteria for being returned to their classroom programme. The average time was 13 to 14 weeks. The length of time was determined by the needs and learning rates of particular children. It should be stressed that this is an *average* length of time in tuition; individual children needed much more time in the programme.

Number of lessons and length
The arrangements that teachers made for lessons varied from child to child and from teacher to teacher. Three teachers used a 40 minute lesson most of the time and others used a short and a long lesson, one of 30 minutes and a second of 10 minutes later in the day. All lessons were transformed into a standard 40 minute lesson equivalent for Tables A-C, pages 74 to 79. However Table 1 shows the variations used by the five teachers.

What Reading Progress Was Made?

The programme differed from most remedial programmes: it was a very *early intervention,* the instruction was *individual, intensive,* and *consistent,* the reading recovery teacher *aimed to accelerate* the child's progress, and she also aimed to make the child as *independent* of her tuition as possible. We were unable to correct for the fact that teachers and principals gained enthusiasm as the programme began to show results and that teachers worked very hard to get results. The final testing, however, was completed by independent outsiders.

Individual progress data
a)   Improvement occurred for children who received tuition. Details of individual progress are provided in Tables A-C.

Progress can be seen by inspection of the Book Level data for

• the shifts in book level by title or
• the number of book steps gained or
• the gains in Stanine scores for book level.

All children in tuition gained in reading skill and most improved markedly over their level at entry. As they read the listed books with over 90 percent accuracy (and this was checked carefully) any gain in book level made it more likely that the child would be able to work effectively with a class reading group.

b)   Table A shows the progress of the 53 D children who received an average of 14 weeks of tuition and then returned to their classrooms for an average of 12 weeks before the final testing (i.e. the D group were Discontinued and Followed-up). Shifts in Stanine scores occurred in the programme and follow-up, but gain scores were higher during the programme.

c)   A comparison between Tables B and C shows the differences between the 42 children who were judged to need further help at the end of the year (Prog. or Programme group) and the 27 who were ready to survive in their class group (Dd or Discontinued but not followed-up). The Programme children were at lower levels and had made less gain, on the average. For all analyses the D and Dd groups were combined, except for the study of what happened during the follow-up period.

d)   The only children in the age cohort for whom the programme may have been unsuitable are described here.

• Four Pacific Island children had insufficient English Language to understand the instructions of the Diagnostic Survey tests.

• The school nurse described one Indian child as having flaccid cerebral palsy. She made very little progress in the programme and was referred for psychological assessment.

• Two children were helped by the programme but were also seen by or referred to the Education Department Psychological Service as possibly needing placements in special classes for children of low intelligence; see Table C (child TS and child FC).

Within-group changes
The mean test scores of all three groups (Discontinued, Programme and Other) increased from initial to final testing (an average of 6 months) on Book Level, Reading Vocabulary, Dictation, and Letter Identification so that statistically-significant differences were recorded ($p < .01$); see Table 2. Writing Vocabulary was not administered initially to the Other group because the teachers did not have time to give the test at that point in their programme,

Initial and Final Test — Scores

Test	Group	Test Time	N	Mean	SD	Sm	t test[1] of differences	Correlation of initial and final test
Book Level	Discontinued	1	80	6.33	3.67	0.41	25.80	0.53*
		2	80	18.53	3.96	0.44		
	Programme	1	42	2.48	1.61	0.25	15.12	0.48*
		2	42	8.21	2.76	0.43		
	Other	1	160	12.54	5.86	0.46	22.12	0.64*
		2	160	20.86	5.47	0.43		
Reading Vocabulary	Discontinued	1	80	9.25	9.32	1.04	4.09	0.42*
		2	80	27.63	6.46	0.72		
	Programme	1	42	4.76	2.96	0.46	14.28	0.47*
		2	42	14.76	5.20	0.80		
	Other	1	160	24.03	16.78	1.33	19.18	0.74*
		2	160	33.53	11.51	0.91		
Concepts About Print	Discontinued	1	80	13.86	2.78	0.31	18.14	0.35*
		2	80	19.79	2.34	0.26		
	Programme	1	42	10.90	2.89	0.45	16.05	0.71*
		2	42	16.00	2.45	0.38		
	Other	1	160	16.83	3.43	0.27	5.73	0.64*
		2	160	17.41	3.77	0.30		
Letter Identification	Discontinued	1	80	37.20	13.52	1.51	9.92	0.14
		2	80	51.55	3.20	0.36		
	Programme	1	42	23.67	14.39	2.22	12.78	0.72*
		2	42	43.29	9.59	1.48		
	Other	1	160	49.06	8.67	0.69	3.91	0.55*
		2	160	50.74	6.30	0.50		
Writing Vocabulary	Discontinued	1	80	10.38	5.80	0.65	17.67	0.18
		2	80	45.69	14.24	1.59		
	Programme	1	42	5.64	2.90	0.45	14.92	0.47*
		2	42	24.05	9.21	1.42		
	Other	1		(Not administered)				
		2	160	48.19	21.76	1.72		
Dictation	Discontinued	1	80	15.44	7.83	0.88	21.39	0.31*
		2	80	33.24	2.97	0.33		
	Programme	1	42	8.29	7.31	1.13	17.31	0.62*
		2	42	24.52	6.53	1.01		
	Other	1	160	27.70	8.59	0.68	6.50	0.65*
		2	160	32.96	5.82	0.46		

1 All t-tests are above 2.69 and are significant.
* Correlations that were significantly above zero at the p<.01 level have an asterisk.

Table 2

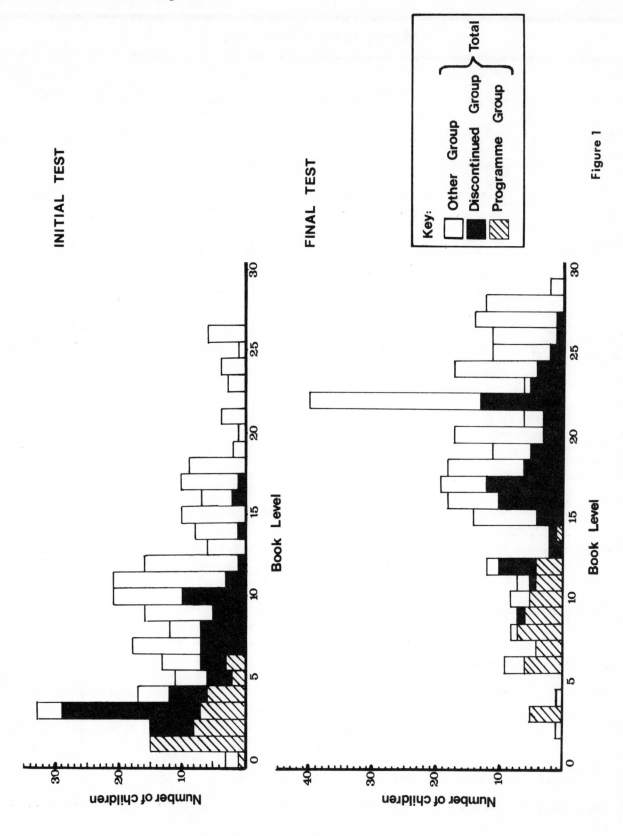

Figure 1

Gain Scores for all Measures
(with t-tests for significant differences between groups)

Test	Group	N	Mean	SD	SEm	t i
Book Level	Discontinued	80	2.84	1.13	0.13	4.62*
	Programme	42	2.00	0.80	0.22	0.29
	Other	160	2.06	1.20	1.11	
Reading Vocabulary	Discontinued	80	2.76	1.01	0.11	5.30*
	Programme	42	1.69	0.87	0.13	0.94
	Other	160	1.89	1.23	0.11	
Concepts About Print	Discontinued	80	2.99	1.51	0.17	9.65*
	Programme	42	2.14	1.00	0.15	4.83*
	Other	160	1.19	1.14	0.13	
Letter Identification	Discontinued	80	2.33	1.36	0.15	5.47*
	Programme	42	1.83	0.93	0.14	2.45
	Other	160	1.34	1.17	0.11	
Writing Vocabulary	Discontinued	80	4.15	1.28	0.14	9.06*
	Programme	42	2.00	1.17	0.18	
	Other	(Not administered)				
Dictation	Discontinued	80	2.71	1.14	0.13	8.29*
	Programme	42	2.14	0.95	0.15	3.99*
	Other	160	1.38	1.11	0.10	

* t-test indicates a significant difference between groups.

Table 3

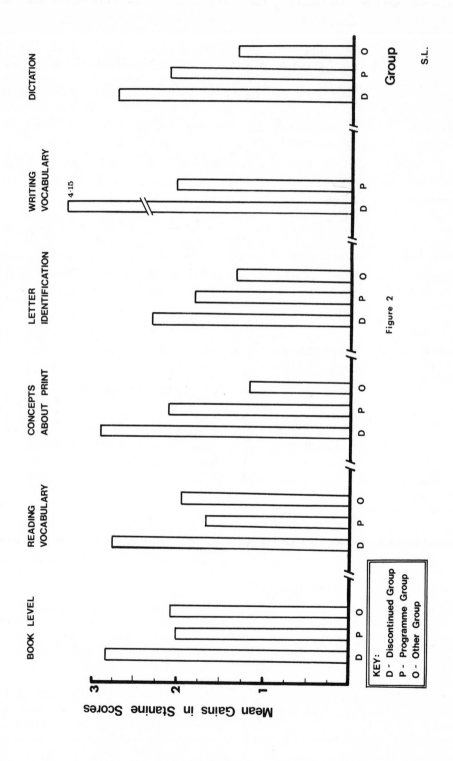

Figure 2

but significant differences were found for both tutored groups.

Figure 1 shows the position of D, Prog. and Other groups on Book Level at initial and final testing. The Reading Vocabulary Test (which is not shown here) showed a very similar shift. Despite the very different nature of these measures, one measuring accuracy on text and the other word reading in isolation, the type of change for each group was similar.

The size of the gains
The pooled scores of all children at both testings were normalized by transforming them to a normalized Stanine scale for each test. This would allow comparisons of gains to be made across tests. Groups were compared on the mean gain scores obtained.*(Table 3 and Figure 2.)

The pupils who received individual tuition made gains which equalled or exceeded the gains made by their classmates who showed initially the higher achievement. The following statements refer to the number of Stanines *gained* but they do not imply that the groups were scoring at the same level on the tests.

a) The Discontinued group made higher and significantly different gains than the Other group in all tests. (Writing Vocabulary was not administered to the Other group.) (Table 3 and Figure 2.)

b) The Programme group made gains that were not significantly lower than those of the Other group on Book Level, Reading Vocabulary and Letter Identification and were significantly higher on Concepts About Print and Dictation.

c) The Discontinued group made significantly higher gains than the Programme pupils on Writing Vocabulary.

Progress in the programme and during a follow-up period
For 53 of the 80 in the Discontinued group there was a period after tuition when they worked in groups back in their classrooms. These children were tested three times:

1   at entry to the programme
2   at exit from the programme
3   at the end of the year.

This allowed for comparisons of the gains that occurred to be made

• within the programme   (1-2)

---

* Note that children in the Other group who were competent at the initial test and who gained Stanine scores of 6 or above at that time were excluded from the comparison as it could be argued that they had little room to shift on a 1-9 Stanine scale. This did in fact happen. Their exclusion from the analysis was a conservative approach to the data.

• after the programme   (2-3)
• across both phases   (1-3)

The progress of the Total group, the Other group, the Programme group and this Discontinued group of 53 is shown in Figure 3 for these phases of the study.* It is evident that

1   The Discontinued group
    a) gained mostly during the programme
    b) continued to gain after the programme
    c) moved to or above the Total group mean by the end of the year.

2   The Programme group
    a) had initial scores that were much lower than the first group, the Discontinued group, which was a sampling difference probably due to chance (see below)
    b) gained during the programme at rates which appear to be comparable to that of the Discontinued children, on all tests (compare the slopes of the lines for the first two points of the Discontinued group with the slope of the lines for the Programme group)
    c) were not ready to leave the programme after an average time of 13 weeks in tuition.

These findings are supported by the analyses in Table 4 and 5.

Was the treatment effective?
What answers can be given to the research question about progress?

There is reason to believe that the Discontinued and Programme groups should be seen as examples of better and poorer samples that might be drawn from the bottom third of any distribution of 6-year-old readers. The progress of the 53 Discontinued and Followed-up group may be better than one would usually predict and that of the Programme group may be rather poorer as they had unusually low beginning scores. This was probably a chance sampling difference as each child entered the study in an order determined by his/her birth date and Discontinued children were merely those who entered school earlier in the year than the Programme children.

1   **Educationally important gains**
    All children improved over their own initial scoring levels (see Tables A-C, for test score gains but particularly for shifts in Book Level).

---

* The Dd group of 27 children who were ready for discontinuing at the end of the year have been omitted from these comparisons merely to achieve a clear report.

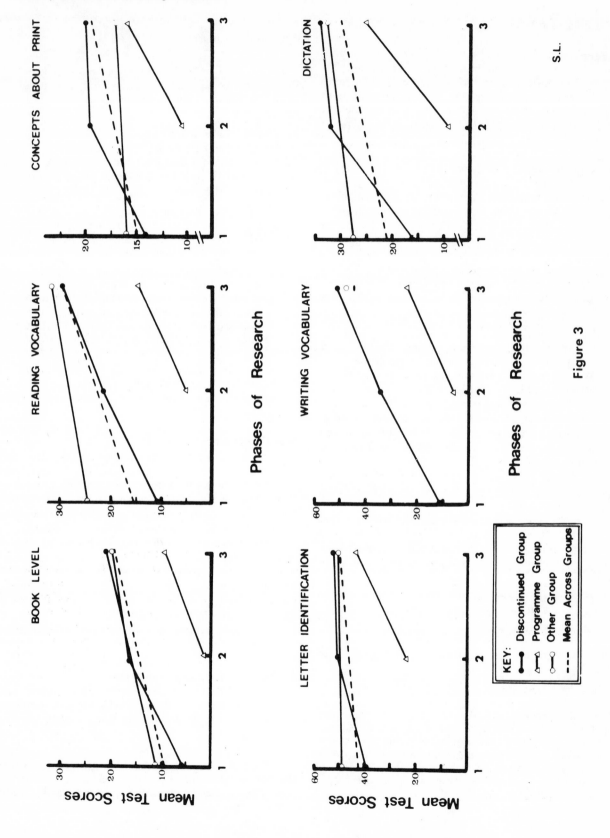

Figure 3

Correlation Between Initial and Final Scores
(as predicted tutoring lowered the relationships)

Group	Phase	Book Level	Reading Vocabulary
No Tutoring			
Other	1-3	0.64	0.74
D	2-3	0.84	0.73
Tutoring			
D	1-2	0.54	0.63
Programme	2-3	0.48	0.47
Total	1-3	0.72	0.68

Table 4

Difference Scores Between Predicted and Final Levels for Discontinued, Programme, and Other Groups in Book Level and Reading Vocabulary

Group	Book Level			Reading Vocabulary		
	Mean	SD	Sm	Mean	SD	Sm
Other	0.14	4.26	0.34	0.94	7.69	0.61
Discontinued with follow-up	2.61	2.95	0.41	4.19	4.74	0.65
Both Discontinued groups	2.34	3.44	0.38	2.26	5.16	0.57
Programme	−5.02	2.45	0.38	−6.56	4.50	0.69

Table 5

t-tests of Group Comparisons on Difference Scores

Group	Book Level		Reading Vocabulary	
	Other	Programme	Other	Programme
Discontinued >	*	*	*	*
Both Discontinued Groups >	*	*	ns	*

* t-test was significant at .01 level.

Table 6

2   Gains in relation to the total age cohort

a) The Programme children, despite a fast rate of progress from low initial scores were still in the bottom third of the age cohort (see Figures 1-3 and Table 3). Further time in the programme may have altered this given the rate and direction of change shown in Figure 3.

b) The Discontinued children made accelerated progress towards the mean performance level of the group on all variables and were able to sustain normal rates of progress after their return to the classroom programme over an average period of 12 weeks (Figure 3).

3   Correlations between initial and final scores

For the Total group the correlation between initial and final scores for Book Level was 0.72 and for Reading Vocabulary 0.68. If the individual tuition was effective it would upset the initial ordering of children and allow some to progress faster than others. Sub-group comparisons of correlations in Table 4 suggest that this may have occurred. In particular when the Discontinued group in Phase 1-2 is compared with Phase 2-3 the correlations suggest that tutoring had the effect of producing a lower correlation in Phase 1-2 (r = 0.54) but that individuals within the group maintained their positions when the programme ended, in Phase 2-3 (r = 0.84).

4   Regression to the mean

Statistically one would predict that, over a period of time, through the natural process of regression to the mean, pupils who score lowest in the first test tend to make the greatest gain.

For each child a prediction of gain was made from initial achievement and the Total group correlation. Difference scores were calculated for the difference between the predicted final score* and the actual final score and t-tests of the difference between the mean differences were calculated.

The results of this analysis, in Table 5, support the conclusion that the gains made by the Discontinued group were significantly greater than the gains of Other and Programme groups after a correction for regression for the mean had been applied.

* $Y^1 = r(\frac{\sigma y}{\sigma x}(X-M_x) + My)$ Guilford, 1965, p.368.

$r^1 = r(\frac{\sigma y}{\sigma x}(X-M_x) + My)$

Discussion

Educationally important gains were made by all children receiving individual tuition. A strong case has been made for the statistical signifcance of the greater gain made by the Discontinued children who were judged to be ready to survive in their classroom programmes, over their initially superior classmates.

These gains were achieved by experienced teachers without academic training in the theory behind the procedures. They were achieved in a field trial, in schools that varied in size and in the type of children who entered the school. And they occurred in programmes in which the teachers had considerable organizational freedom.

On the basis of these results an in-service programme will be arranged in 1979 to try out these procedures in 49 volunteer schools in the Auckland area with a class teacher freed for individual teaching for two hours every day. This is calculated to reach 1000 children in the year.

However, while the principles upon which this programme was based; *individual, intensive, consistent* tuition, *applied very early* to provide a second chance for children finding it difficult to learn to read; it is assumed that schools will have different needs for such programmes. The results from the five schools in the 1978 programme lead to the conclusion that the important variables to consider in calculating teacher-time for such work would be

- the number of children in the junior school
- the attainment levels in the school
- the language problems of children
- the mobility problems of the population
- the social problems of the district.

Even in small schools .5 of a teacher would be usefully employed. Most schools would need 1 to 1.5 teachers. A large school with language, home and mobility problems could utilize 2 teachers on reading recovery work alone.

This would not be a luxury service but rather an economy strategy. Effort and money invested to de-confuse confused children and put them in a position to profit from subsequent education would undercut some of the reading difficulty problem, and cut the costs of remediation in the upper primary school. It would also separate out the children who have not made a satisfactory start from the children who have marked difficulty because of some organic problem. Clinic tuition from trained experts will still be needed for the latter group but they will also profit from the 'reading recovery' programme because they would be identified by 6:6 years at the latest.

The administrative change that is required is simple.

Schools need to be staffed to allow for a set number of individual teaching hours in each teacher's week, say, conservatively, two. Principals could then be allowed to organize for the use of such time in a way that was most suitable for that school.

It is suspected that oral language and mathematics may also have a claim on individual teaching time with a view to accelerating the language-limited or maths-confused child to a point where he/she can profit better from what the school offers. To make such things possible it may be appropriate to think of individual recovery programmes in the Junior School as follows:

First year   Oral Language
Second year   Reading
Third year   Mathematics

It must be stated that the effect of the programme was unlikely to have arisen merely from individual tutoring time. The reading recovery procedures

• allowed for differential treatment of children as all children did not follow the same programme
• arose from the study of normal progress in the New Zealand programme and aimed to fit children to survive in that programme
• were applied by experienced teachers without special training but with an in-service discussion group for support
• were clearly articulated in line with a body of theory about the (normal) reading process that is supported by recognized experts (Goodman, 1976; Smith, 1978)
• were monitored by assessment techniques that were applied by the teachers and were sensitive to the actual behaviours being learnt and being used by the child in reading.

Perhaps the main reason why good teachers made good theory and procedures work with poor learners was that close attention was paid to professional and institutional factors that might affect the programme. The support provided by Principals, STJC's, the Department of Education, in particular the Deputy Senior Inspector of Primary Schools in Auckland, Mr Walbran, and to two gifted tutors of teachers, Sue Robinson and Barbara Watson are acknowledged. But if the change one attempts to bring about is incompatible with the system the project will not succeed. In this case what we tried to do fitted comfortably into the educational system and offered every gain to those who supported it. Perhaps that is the main reason why it worked well.

Preventive intervention programmes are difficult research areas. It is difficult to show that what is prevented would, in fact, ever have occurred in the treated subjects. And more subjects will be treated than may eventually need the programme if the problem is allowed to develop to an advanced stage. The reported research falls into the category of secondary prevention, based on the earliest effective intervention for groups of children. Earlier isolation of children having reading problems will produce too many false diagnoses, given the present state of knowledge, and the reliability and validity of techniques.

There may be some features of the present research which have more general application for preventive intervention in the social sciences.

• Definitive descriptive research mapping helpful and harmful sequences was carried out in intensive, short-term longitudinal research.
• Behavioural data was used even though the conceptualization of the problem or its treatment may not necessarily have been in behavioural terms.
• Intervention techniques were designed to bring about a change from the harmful to the helpful sequence.
• The outcomes of intervention were tested by recording a continuing sequence of helpful behaviour responses after intervention activities had terminated.
• The direction, extent and duration of the change were subjected to research analysis.

References and Further Reading

Clay, Marie M., 'Emergent Reading Behaviour'. Unpubl. doctoral dissertation, University of Auckland Library, 1966.

Clay, Marie M., 'The reading behaviour of five year old children: a research report'. *N.Z. Journal of Educational Studies.* 2 (1), 1967, pp 11-31.

Clay, Marie M., 'Reading errors and self-correction behaviour'. *British Journal of Educational Psychology,* 39, 1969. pp 47-56.

Clay, Marie M., 'Research on language and reading in Pakeha and Polynesian children', in D. K. Bracken and E. Malmquist (eds.), *Improving Reading Ability Around The World,* International Reading Association, Newark, Delaware, 1970.

Clay, Marie M., *Reading: The Patterning of Complex Behaviour.* Second Edition. Heinemann Educational Books, Auckland, 1979.

Clay, Marie M., *What Did I Write?* Heinemann Educational Books, Auckland, 1975.

De Hirsch, Katrina; Jansky, J. and Longford, W. J. *Predicting the Failing Reader,* Harper and Row, New York, 1966.

Elkonin, D. B., USSR. In Downing, John. *Comparative Reading: Cross-National Studies of Behaviour and Processes in Reading and Writing.* Macmillan, New York, 1975.

Fernald, Grace M., *Remedial Techniques in Basic School Subjects,* McGraw-Hill, New York, 1943.

Goodacre, Elizabeth, *Children and Learning to Read,* Routledge and Kegan Paul, London, 1971.

Goodman, K.S. 'Analysis of oral reading miscues: applied psycholinguistics', *Reading Research Quarterly,* 1, 1969, pp 9-30.

Guildford, J. P., *Fundamental Statistics in Psychology and Education,* Fourth Edition, McGraw-Hill, New York, 1965.

Hildreth, G. Early writing as an aid to reading. *Elementary English,* 40, 1964, 15-20.

Hooton, Margaret, *The First Reading and Writing Book,* Heinemann Educational Books, Auckland, 1976.

Lyman, H.B., *Test Scores and What They Mean,* Prentice-Hall, Englewood Cliffs, New Jersey, 1963.

McLeod J., *The Gap Reading Comprehension Test,* Heinemann Educational Books, Melbourne, 1965.

Neale, Marie D., *The Neale Analysis of Reading Ability,* Macmillan, London, 1958.

Reid, Jessie, 'Learning to think about reading', *Educational Research,* 9, (1), 1966 pp 56-62.

Robinson, Susan M. Predicting Early Reading Progress. Unpubl. M.A. thesis, University of Auckland Library, 1973.

Smith, F., *Understanding Reading*, Second Edition, Holt Rhinehart and Winston, New York, 1978.

Strang, Ruth., *The Diagnostic Teaching of Reading,* McGraw-Hill, New York, 1969.

Appendix

SUMMARY   OF   RUNNING   RECORD

Name: _____   Date: _____ D.of B. _____._____   Age: _____ yrs _____ mths

SUMMARY OF RUNNING RECORD

	TEXT TITLES		RUNNING WORDS ERROR	ERROR RATE	ACCURACY	SELF-CORRECTION
1.	Easy	_____	_____	1: _____	_____ %	1 : _____
2.	Instructional	_____	_____	1: _____	_____ %	1 : _____
3.	Hard	_____	_____	1: _____	_____ %	1 : _____

Directional
Movement _____

ANALYSIS OF ERRORS   Cues used and cues neglected

Easy _____

Instructional _____
        _____

Hard _____
        _____

CROSS CHECKING ON CUES

Page		E	SC	

Page		E	SC	

DIAGNOSTIC SUMMARY SHEET

Recommended for survey checks after one year of instruction

Name: _____ Date: _____ D.of B. _____ Age: ____ yrs _____ mths

SUMMARY OF RUNNING RECORD

TEXT TITLES	RUNNING WORDS ERROR	ERROR RATE	ACCURACY	SELF-CORRECTION
1. Easy _____	_____	1: _____	_____ %	1 : _____
2. Instructional _____	_____	1: _____	_____ %	1 : _____
3. Hard _____	_____	1: _____	_____ %	1 : _____

Directional
Movement _____

ANALYSIS OF ERRORS Cues used and cues neglected

Easy _____

Instructional _____

_____

Hard _____

_____

CROSS CHECKING ON CUES

_____

LETTER IDENTIFICATION

	$\overline{54}$

CONCEPTS ABOUT PRINT

	$\overline{24}$

WORD TEST (Clay)   LIST 1 _____ LIST 2 _____ LIST 3 _____

OTHER WORD TEST.   _____
(SCHONELL, BURT-VERNON

$\overline{15}$	$\overline{30}$

WRITING SAMPLE	WRITING VOCABULARY	DICTATION	STORY	SPELLING
Language :				
Message :				
Direction:				

USEFUL STRATEGIES ON TEXT:

PROBLEM STRATEGIES ON TEXT:

USEFUL STRATEGIES ON WORDS:

PROBLEM STRATEGIES ON WORDS:

USEFUL STRATEGIES ON LETTERS:

PROBLEM STRATEGIES ON LETTERS:

SUMMARY:

Signature: _____

PROCESSING ANALYSIS SUMMARY SHEET

RECORD OF WORD SOLVING PROGRESS

Name _____

Reader _____

Date _____

ANALYSIS OF WORD SOLVING

ANALYSIS OF ERRORS

Text Count A or of B or word C Errors	Acceptable Graphic Cues						Syntax Accept able	Semantics Accept able	Audible analysis		Silent analysis (pause)	Self Correction			Count of Words Solved
	Zero	Reversal	First	Last	Middle	First 2 elements + last different	1 element different			1st sound	1st sounds	1st syllable		Syntax	Meaning	Sounds 1st Last Middle

Accuracy

TEXT A (Easy) _____

TEXT B (Instructional) _____

TEXT C (Hard) _____

Calculation   and   Conversion   Tables

Error Rate	Percent Accuracy
1 : 200	99.5
1 : 100	99
1 : 50	98
1 : 35	97
1 : 25	96
1 : 20	95
1 : 17	94
1 : 14	93
1 : 12.5	92
1 : 11.75	91
1 : 10	90
1 : 9	89
1 : 8	87.5
1 : 7	85.5
1 : 6	83
1 : 5	80
1 : 4	75
1 : 3	66
1 : 2	50

CALCULATIONS

RW   =   Running Words

E   =   Errors

SC   =   Self-corrections

Error Rate

Running words

   Errors

e.g. $\dfrac{150}{15}$ =   Ratio 1 : 10

Accuracy

$100 - \dfrac{E}{RW} \times \dfrac{100}{1}$

$100 - \dfrac{15}{150} \times \dfrac{100}{1}$ %

= 90%

Self-Correction Rate

$\dfrac{E + SC}{SC}$

$\dfrac{15 + 5}{5}$ =   Ratio 1 : 4

CONCEPTS ABOUT PRINT SCORE SHEET

Date: _____

Name: _____ Age: _____   TEST SCORE

Recorder: _____ Date of Birth: _____   STANINE GROUP

PAGE	SCORE	ITEM	COMMENT
Cover		1. Front of book	
2/3		2. Print contains message	
4/5		3. Where to start	
4/5		4. Which way to go	
4/5		5. Return sweep to left	
4/5		6. Word by word matching	
6		7. First and last concept	
7		8. Bottom of picture	
8/9		9. Begin 'The' (Sand) or 'I' (Stones) bottom line, top OR turn book	
10/11		10. Line order altered	
12/13		11. Left page before right	
12/13		12. One change in word order	
12/13		13. One change in letter order	
14/15		14. One change in letter order	
14/15		15. Meaning of ?	
16/17		16. Meaning of full stop	
16/17		17. Meaning of comma	
16/17		18. Meaning of quotation marks	
16/17		19. Locate M m H h (Sand) OR T t B b (Stones)	
18/19		20. Reversible words was, no	
20		21. Show one letter, show two letters	
20		22. Just one word: 2 words	
20		23. First and last letter of word	
20		24. Capital letters	

LETTER IDENTIFICATION SHEET

Date: _____

Name: _____   Age: _____   TEST SCORE | /54

Recorder: _____   Date of birth _____   STANINE GROUP

	A	S	Word	I.R.		A	S	Word	I.R.
A									
F					f				
K					k				
P					p				
W					w				
Z					z				
B					b				
H					h				
O					o				
J					j				
U					u				
					a				
C					c				
Y					y				
L					l				
Q					q				
M					m				
D					d				
N					n				
S					s				
X					x				
I					i				
E					e				
G					g				
R					r				
V					v				
T					t				
TOTALS									
			Grand Totals						

Confusions:

Letters Unknown:

Comments:

Recording:

A   Alphabet response
       Tick

S   Letter sound response
       Tick

Word   Record the word the
       child gives

IR   Incorrect response
       Record what child
       says

WORD   TEST   SCORE   SHEET

Use any <u>one</u> list of words.

Date: _____

Name: _____   Age: _____

	TEST SCORE	/ / 15
	STANINE GROUP	

Recorder: _____   Date of birth: _____

Recording: _____ Record Incorrect Responses

LIST A	LIST B	LIST C
I	and	Father
Mother	to	come
are	will	for
here	look	a
me	he	you
shouted	up	at
am	like	school
with	in	went
car	where	get
children	Mr	we
help	going	they
not	big	ready
too	go	this
meet	let	boys
away	on	please

COMMENT:

DICTATION TEST SHEET

Date _____

Name: _____   Age: _____   TEST SCORE | /37 |

STANINE GROUP | |

Recorder: _____   Date of birth: _____

(Fold heading under before child uses sheet)

- -

WRITING VOCABULARY TEST SHEET

Date _____

Name: _____   Age: _____

TEST SCORE

[ ]

STANINE GROUP

[ ]

Recorder: _____   Date of birth: _____

(Fold heading under before child uses sheet)

- -

LESSON   PLAN

ENTER DATE:

NAME

READER	REVISION	WORD STUDY	STRUCTURAL ELEMENT	LETTER FORMATION	LETTER IDENTIFICATION

SPATIAL CONCEPTS	SEQUENCING	WRITING	ANALYSIS	COMMENT

RECOMMENDATIONS FOR DISCONTINUING TUTORING   Name:_____

Date: _____

1.   SETTING   (Same class, new class, book level, teacher's reaction, size of
                group etc.)

2.   SURVIVAL   (Detail what behaviours will ensure coping in group instruction.)

3.   RUNNING RECORD ANALYSIS

4.   COMMENT ON IMPROVEMENTS SINCE PREVIOUS STUDY SUMMARY AND PREDICTIONS

Signed: _____

Retested: _____   Date: _____

Recommendation approved: _____   Date: _____

REVIEW PROGRAMME:

STANINE SCORE SUMMARY SHEET

"READY TO READ" WORD TEST

320 urban children aged 5:0 - 7:0 in 1968	Stanine Score	1	2	3	4	5	6	7	8	9
	Test Score	0	0	1	2-15	6-12	13-14	-	15	-

282 urban children aged 6:0 - 7:3 in 1978	Stanine Score	1	2	3	4	5	6	7	8	9
	Test Score	0-1	2-5	6-9	10-12	13-14	-	15	-	-

LETTER IDENTIFICATION

320 urban children aged 5:0 - 7:0 in 1968	Stanine Score	1	2	3	4	5	6	7	8	9
	Test Score	-	0	2-7	8-25	26-47	48-52	53	54	-

282 urban children aged 6:0 - 7:3 in 1978	Stanine Score	1	2	3	4	5	6	7	8	9
	Test Score	0-13	14-28	29-43	44-49	50-52	53	-	54	-

CONCEPTS ABOUT PRINT

320 urban children aged 5:0 - 7:0 in 1968	Stanine Score	1	2	3	4	5	6	7	8	9
	Test Score	0	1-4	5-7	8-11	12-14	15-17	18-20	21-22	23-24

282 urban children aged 6:0 - 7:3 in 1978	Stanine Score	1	2	3	4	5	6	7	8	9
	Test Score	0-9	10-11	12-13	14-16	17-18	19	20-21	11	23-24

WRITING VOCABULARY

282 urban children aged 6:0 - 7:3 in 1978	Stanine Score	1	2	3	4	5	6	7	8	9
	Test Score	0-13	14-19	20-28	29-35	36-45	46-55	56-70	71-80	81-

DICTATION

282 urban children aged 6:0 - 7:3 in 1978	Stanine Score	1	2	3	4	5	6	7	8	9
	Test Score	0-3	4-9	10-17	18-27	28-31	32-35	36-37	-	-

Index